BRIDGING THE GAP

Between Who God Says You Are and How You Live

Robin Urban

Benchmark Press
Printed in the United States of America

CONTENTS

ABOUT THE AUTHOR

Robin Urban is a wife, mother, and grandmother residing in Toledo, Ohio, where she serves on the teaching team at Foundation Stone Church in Northwood. A graduate of the University of Toledo with a degree in History, she writes from the heart of a believer who has discovered the transformative power of God's grace through His Word. Her passion is helping fellow Christians bridge the gap between knowing who they are in Christ and experiencing that reality in daily life. When not teaching or writing, Robin pursues her love of weightlifting and CrossFit.

ACKNOWLEDGEMENTS

"I didn't discover the truths in this book in a vacuum — they came through the faithful teaching and encouragement of people God placed in my life.

I'm grateful for the pastors, teachers, and ministers whose proclamation of the gospel and grace has shaped how I see God's Word. Their faithful preaching week after week has deepened my understanding of the New Covenant in ways I'm still discovering.

But most of all, I'm thankful for my husband, Andrew. He's listened to every undeveloped idea, endured every theological rabbit trail, and encouraged me when I doubted whether I had anything worth saying. This book exists because he believed in the message long before I had the courage to write it down.

To each of you: thank you for directing me toward Jesus. Any truth in these pages comes from God's Word alone. Any clarity comes from the Holy Spirit's work. I'm just grateful God let me share it."

INTRODUCTION

The Question Every Believer Asks

Here's the question that haunts every honest believer: *If I'm really a new creation, why do I still struggle with the same issues? Why does anxiety still grip me? Why do I fall back into old patterns of thinking and speaking? If old things have passed away, why do they keep showing up in my life?*

Friend, let me tell you something incredible: you are not who you used to be. The moment you gave your life to Jesus, everything changed. As 2 Corinthians 5:17 proclaims, "If anyone is in Christ, he is a new creation; old things have passed away; behold, all things have become new."

That's not just a promise for heaven. It's the truth of who you are right now in Christ.

When Jesus died on the cross, your old self, the one burdened by sin, shame, and failure, was crucified with Him *(Galatians 2:20- 'I have been crucified with Christ; it is no longer I who live, but Christ lives in me; and the life which I now live in the flesh I live by faith in the Son of God, who loved me and gave Himself for me")*. In God's eyes, you're seen through the lens of His Son's righteousness, pure and complete.

If you have ever asked that question. If you know theologically that you're righteous in Christ, but practically you still feel dominated by the old nature. If you've been told you're a new creation, but don't know how to actually walk in that reality. If you're tired of the gap between who the Bible says you are and who you experience yourself to be, *then this book is for you!*

The Gap Between Identity and Experience

Here's what's true: You are perfect in Christ eternally. God sees you as righteous, holy, and completely accepted. Your position before Him is established, and secure.

But here's what's also true: You're learning to walk in that reality daily. And that learning process, how to live from your new identity rather than your old patterns, is where most believers get entangled.

It's like getting married and legally changing your name. On paper, you're immediately Mrs. Johnson. Your driver's license says so. The government agrees. But you still accidentally sign checks as Miss Smith for the next six months, and your brain short-circuits every time someone calls you by your new name at the grocery store. You ARE Mrs. Johnson; legally, officially, permanently. You're just learning to live like Mrs. Johnson. That's exactly where you are as a new creation.

It's not that you need to become a new creation. You already are one. The question is: How do you walk as the new person God created you to be? How do you access the divine power that's already been granted to you? How do you experience in daily life what's already true in eternal reality?

That's the gap this book bridges.

The Pattern That Changes Everything

What if I told you there's a simple, biblical pattern woven throughout Scripture that shows exactly how transformation happens? A pattern that's not about trying harder or being more disciplined, but about positioning yourself to receive what God has already provided?

This pattern appears in the story of Cornelius in Acts 10. It shows up in the life of Abraham. It's paramount in the story of Joshua, Caleb, and the Ten Spies. It's explained by Paul in Romans and Galatians. It's the mechanism Jesus Himself described when He talked about abiding in the vine.

The pattern is this: **hear God's Word, believe it, speak it, and receive what He's provided.**

That's it. That's how the Christian life was designed to work. Not through striving, but through receiving. Not through performance, but through faith in what's already been accomplished. Not by trying to become who you should be, but by learning to walk in who you already are. Remember, you are a new creation in Christ Jesus. That's it. It is as simple and as difficult as that. The problem begins, however, when we forget that simple truth and begin trying to focus on how to correct certain aspects of the old man. The old man is dead. Leave him behind.

What This Book Promises

In these pages, you'll discover:

- **The biblical pattern** (hear-believe-speak-receive) that appears throughout Scripture and shows how transformation truly works
- **Why your new identity isn't just a legal status in heaven's records** - it's a lived reality you can walk in daily.
- **What Jesus accomplished at the cross** makes every promise in God's Word accessible to you right now
- **How God's Word itself does the transforming work** when you position yourself to receive it (you don't make it work; it works in you)
- **The difference between Old Covenant living** ("commandments to do") **and New Covenant living** ("words to believe")
- **Practical application** of this pattern to every area where you need transformation: anxiety, sin patterns, sickness, lack, broken relationships

This isn't another spiritual discipline to master or program to complete. This is how grace actually operates. This is the divine power principle described in 2 Peter 1:3: "His divine power has granted to us all things that pertain to life and godliness, through the knowledge of Him."

You have access to everything you need. The question is: How do you access it?

Why This Message Matters Now

We live in a time when believers have more access to the Bible than any generation in history, like apps, podcasts, online sermons, and many translations. Yet many Christians remain, still dominated by the old patterns they thought salvation would eliminate.

The problem isn't a lack of information. The problem is not understanding the mechanism. We've been told *what* we are (new creations) without being shown *how* to walk in it. We know the promises, but don't know how to receive them. We have the truth, but don't know the pattern.

This book reveals that process. Not as something new or novel, but as something ancient that's been there all along, waiting to be reclaimed.

How to Use This Book

Think of this as a field manual, not a one-time read. You'll return to it whenever you notice the gap growing between your identity and your experience. Keep it accessible for those moments when old patterns reappear, when you catch yourself living from the flesh instead of the Spirit, or when you need to remember how transformation actually works.

Each chapter ends with key Scripture passages that capture the core truth. These aren't just nice verses to glance at. They are the actual words you'll use to engage the pattern. Read them aloud to crystallize that chapter's key theme. Let them sink into your heart. Come back to them when you need to remember what God has said. As you hear them, believe them, speak them, you'll receive what they promise.

You can read this book alone or discuss it with a small group. The principles work whether you're a new believer or have been walking with Christ for decades. Wherever you are, this pattern will show you how to bridge the gap between your eternal identity and your daily experience.

Grab your Bible to accompany your reading. The Bible is our main text and source material. You'll want to look up verses, see the context, and let God's Word speak directly to you. Don't just take my word for it - verify everything in Scripture.

What Lies Ahead

We'll start with Cornelius's story in Acts 10, where we see the complete pattern in action. Then we'll examine each step:

- **How faith comes** through hearing God's Word (not through trying harder)
- **What it means to believe** when circumstances seem to contradict God's promises
- **Why speaking matters** and how your words cooperate with grace
- **How to receive** what God has already provided through Christ's finished work

Most importantly, you'll discover that you don't have to manufacture transformation through discipline and determination. God's Word itself does the work when you position yourself to receive it. Your role isn't to make it happen—it's to allow it to happen.

My prayer is that as you read these pages, the gap will close. Not because you suddenly get better at Christian living, but because you discover how to access the divine power that's been yours all along. You'll stop trying to become a new creation and start walking as the new creation you already are.

The abundant life Jesus promised isn't someday. It's not after you get your act together. It's available right now through the pattern He's revealed in His Word.

You ready? Let's discover how to *Be* who you already are.

Therefore, if any man be in Christ, he is a new creature:
old things are passed away;
behold, all things are become new.
2 Corinthians 5:17

CHAPTER 1:

THE PATTERN REVEALED - CORNELIUS HEARS THE WORD

In Acts 10, we meet a man whose transformation reveals God's pattern for walking in grace. Cornelius was a Roman centurion, a Gentile living outside God's covenant with Israel. But he wasn't just any Roman soldier. Scripture paints a detailed picture of a man who had everything the world considers admirable, yet lacked the one thing that matters most.

The Good Man Who Wasn't Good Enough

Acts 10:1-2 describes Cornelius as *"a devout man and one who feared God with all his household, who gave alms generously to the people and prayed to God always."* Let's examine what this meant in his cultural context.

As a centurion of the Italian Regiment, Cornelius commanded approximately 100 Roman soldiers. He had achieved a significant military rank, financial security, and social respect. In a time when Romans typically viewed Jews with suspicion or disdain, Cornelius was different. He "feared God," a technical term meaning he was a Gentile who worshiped the God of Israel without fully converting to Judaism.

His devotion was genuine and costly. He gave "alms generously," not just token charity, but substantial financial gifts to help the Jewish poor. This required real sacrifice and demonstrated a heart genuinely stirred by compassion. He "prayed to God always," maintaining consistent spiritual discipline in a pagan military environment where such devotion could have damaged his career prospects.

By every human measure, Cornelius was extraordinary. He was moral, generous, spiritually minded, and respectful toward God's people. If anyone deserved salvation based on good works, it would have been this man. Yet despite all his admirable qualities, something crucial was missing.

God saw Cornelius's seeking heart, but He also knew that good works, even sincere religious devotion, cannot bridge the gap between humanity and Himself. Romans 3:23 declares that *"all have sinned and fall short of the glory of God,"* and Romans 6:23 reminds us that *"the wages of sin is death, but the gift of God is eternal life in Christ Jesus our Lord."*

Cornelius needed what we all need: the grace that comes only through Jesus Christ.

The Power of Hearing

One day, an angel of God appeared to Cornelius in a vision with a message. His instructions were clear and pressing: "Call for one Simon, whose surname is Peter, he shall tell you what to do." Cornelius immediately obeyed, sending servants to Joppa with a specific message for Peter: "Cornelius the centurion, a just man, one who fears God and has a good reputation among all the nation of the Jews, was divinely instructed by a holy angel to summon you to his house, and to hear words from you" (Acts 10:22). Notice what was emphasized: *hear words.* Not more good deeds, not additional religious rituals, not even deeper personal devotion, but hearing God's Word. This sets the foundation for everything that follows.

The emphasis on "hearing words" appears repeatedly in this account. When Peter arrived, Cornelius explained: *"I sent for you immediately, and you have done well to come. Now therefore, we are all present here before God, to hear all the things commanded you by God" (Acts 10:33).*

Picture this scene: Cornelius had gathered his household, relatives, and close friends, probably 20-30 people or more. He'd arranged his schedule, prepared his home, and assembled everyone he cared about for one purpose: to hear God's Word. This wasn't casual religious entertainment; it was a desperate hunger for truth that could only be satisfied by divine revelation.

An entire household positioned itself to hear God's Word, not to perform religious duties or demonstrate their devotion, but to receive what God wanted to give them. This mirrors what Romans 10:17 teaches: "Faith comes by hearing, and hearing by the word of God." Faith doesn't come from trying harder, being more sincere, or performing religious activities more consistently; it comes from exposing your heart to God's truth.

When an angel tells you someone is coming with words for you, you don't just show up; you gather everyone you love because you know this is going to be good. Cornelius positioned his entire household in *eager expectation*, ready to hear whatever God wanted to say. Through that hearing, faith came alive. The same happens when you position yourself to hear God's Word—not out of duty, but with expectancy that what you're about to hear will change everything.

The Message Delivered

When Peter arrived, he didn't give a casual devotional or inspirational talk. He preached the full gospel message about Jesus Christ. Acts 10:34-43 records his powerful presentation, which can be summarized in these key points:

God's Impartiality: Peter began by declaring, *"In truth I perceive that God shows no partiality. But in every nation whoever fears Him and works righteousness is accepted by Him" (vv. 34-35).* This was groundbreaking; salvation wasn't limited to the Jewish nation but was available to all who would receive it.

Jesus's Life and Ministry: Peter testified about *"Jesus of Nazareth, how God anointed Him with the Holy Spirit and with power, who went about doing good and healing all who were oppressed by the devil, for God was with Him" (v. 38).* He established Jesus's credentials as the promised Messiah through His miraculous works.

The Crucifixion and Resurrection: *"Him they killed by hanging on a tree. Him God raised on the third day, and showed Him openly" (vv. 39-40).* Peter didn't gloss over the scandal of the cross or present a diluted version of the gospel. He declared both the horror of Jesus's death and the triumph of His resurrection.

Eyewitness Testimony: Peter emphasized that he and the other apostles were *"witnesses of all things which He did both in the land of the Jews and in Jerusalem"* and that they *"ate and drank with Him after He arose from the dead"* (vv. 39, 41).

This wasn't secondhand information or religious philosophy; it was firsthand testimony from those who had lived with Jesus.

Universal Forgiveness: Peter concluded with the heart of the gospel: *"To Him all the prophets witness that, through His name, whoever believes in Him will receive remission of sins"* (v. 43). This wasn't complicated theology requiring years of study, it was the simple truth that faith in Christ's finished work brings complete forgiveness and new life, without qualification.

What Peter didn't say is critical. He didn't tell Cornelius to try harder, be more religious, or add Christian practices to his already impressive spiritual resume. He proclaimed what Jesus had accomplished and invited Cornelius to receive it by faith. This was pure grace, unmerited favor available to anyone who would believe.

Cornelius and his household heard words about grace, not works. They learned their salvation came through Jesus's sacrifice, not their own efforts. This is the foundation of your new creation identity: you're righteous because of what Jesus did, not because of what you do.

The Response

What happened next was extraordinary and immediate. Acts 10:44 says, "While Peter was still speaking these words, the Holy Spirit fell upon all those who heard the word." Peter hadn't even finished his sermon when God responded to their faith.

They didn't have to wait, pray through, or prove their sincerity. The moment they heard the gospel and believed it in their hearts, God moved. This demonstrates that salvation is entirely God's work in response to simple faith, not a reward for religious performance or spiritual maturity.

Luke records that *"those of the circumcision who believed were astonished, as many as came with Peter, because the gift of the Holy Spirit had been poured out on the Gentiles also"* (v. 45). The Jewish believers were shocked, not because God moved, but because He moved so quickly and powerfully among Gentiles who had no religious pedigree or covenant background.

This reveals something crucial about God's grace: it's not limited by your background, your past, or your previous religious experience. If you can hear God's Word and believe it, you can receive everything He has to offer.

Your past failures don't disqualify you. Your previous disappointments with God don't create a barrier He can't overcome. The years you spent trying and failing to live right don't count against you. God isn't cataloguing your spiritual track record to determine whether you deserve His grace. He's looking at Jesus's finished work to determine what you can receive.

Maybe you've tried to change a hundred times and fallen back into the same patterns. Maybe you've prayed desperate prayers that seemed to go unanswered. Maybe you've been hurt by religious leaders or disillusioned by church experiences. None of that matters now. Grace meets you right where you are, with whatever history you carry, and offers you the same access to God that Cornelius received: hear His Word, believe His promises, and receive what He's freely giving.

God doesn't view your past struggles as obstacles to overcome. He views them as the very reason Jesus came. Your history of trying and failing doesn't make you less qualified for grace; it makes you the perfect candidate. The religious baggage you're carrying, the spiritual exhaustion from years of performance-based Christianity, the guilt over past failures—these aren't barriers to receiving God's promises. They're the exact conditions that demonstrate why grace is so necessary and so powerful.

Cornelius came with an impressive religious resume, yet it wasn't enough. You might come with a resume full of failures, and that's exactly right. Grace doesn't require you to mend your past before approaching God. It invites you to come as you are and discover that your identity isn't based on where you've been, but on who Jesus is and what He's accomplished.

Speaking the Response

Here's where the complete pattern becomes visible. Acts 10:46 records what happened as they believed: "For they heard them speak with tongues and magnify God." Their belief immediately became verbal; they couldn't contain what they had received.

Speaking in tongues was evidence that the Holy Spirit had come upon them, but notice what else they did: they "magnified God." They were enlarging Him, extolling Him, speaking of His greatness. They were declaring God's goodness, His mercy, His power, and His grace.

Picture the scene: a room full of Gentiles who moments before had no covenant relationship with God, now filled with the Holy Spirit, speaking in supernatural languages, and loudly praising God for His goodness. They weren't whispering quiet prayers; they were boldly proclaiming what God had done.

This demonstrates the third part of God's pattern: speaking what you believe. As 2 Corinthians 4:13 says, *"Since we have the same spirit of faith, according to what is written, 'I believed, and therefore I spoke,' we also believe, and therefore speak."*

When God's Word fills your heart, and you believe it, it naturally overflows in your speech. You find yourself declaring His promises, confessing His truth over your circumstances, and magnifying His goodness to others. This isn't forced or artificial; it's the natural response of a heart that has received God's grace.

Their speaking wasn't just an emotional expression; it was a faith-filled declaration. They were encouraging themselves and each other about what God had done. When you speak God's truth, you're not trying to convince Him to act; you're agreeing with what He's already said and done.

The Complete Pattern Revealed

Cornelius's household experienced the complete pattern that every believer can follow:

1. They heard God's Word through Peter's preaching
2. They believed the gospel message in their hearts
3. They spoke in tongues and magnified God
4. They received the Holy Spirit and salvation

This reveals the pattern: hear God's Word, believe it, speak it, and receive what He's provided. This is how Cornelius and his household were transformed, and it's how you can walk in your new creation identity every day.

Notice that they didn't earn this experience through their good works, religious dedication, or spiritual maturity. They positioned themselves to hear God's Word, believed what they heard, spoke their faith, and received God's grace. The transformation was immediate and complete.

Peter's response confirms this: *"Can anyone forbid water, that these should not be baptized who have received the Holy Spirit just as we have?" (v. 47).* He recognized that God had done the same work in these Gentiles that He had done in the Jewish believers at Pentecost, not because they deserved it, but because they believed.

This is the gospel in action. This is the New Covenant functioning exactly as God intended. And this same pattern is available to you for every area of your life where you need God's grace to manifest.

Two Ways to Relate to God

Before we move forward, we need to understand a crucial distinction that Cornelius's story reveals. There are two completely different approaches to relating with God: the Old Covenant mindset of doing as God commands and the New Covenant reality of believing what God has promised and resting in what He has already provided.

The Old Covenant operated through external rules and regulations that demanded compliance. It told you what to do but provided no power to carry it out. "Be holy." "Love perfectly." "Don't sin." These were commandments to obey through human effort and willpower. The problem? No one could keep them perfectly, and partial obedience isn't obedience at all under the law.

The New Covenant operates under believing what God says; the truth that transforms from the inside out. Instead of commanding you to change through effort, it reveals what Christ has already done and invites you to receive it by faith. This is exactly what we saw with Cornelius. Peter didn't give him a list of behaviors to modify. He proclaimed what Jesus accomplished, and transformation followed naturally.

This distinction matters because it determines your entire approach to dealing with sin, sickness, depression, anxiety, financial pressure, relationship struggles, everything. The "do" mindset says: "Try harder. Be more disciplined. Work up more faith. Force yourself to change." This approach always fails because you're trying to accomplish through human effort what only God's grace can achieve.

The "believe" mindset says: "Hear what God says. Believe His promises. Speak His truth. Receive what He's provided." This approach works because you're cooperating with divine power rather than striving in your own strength. The hear-believe-speak-receive pattern isn't just another method; it's how the New Covenant functions. It's the key to victory over everything that tries to dominate your life.

Cornelius and his household experienced this firsthand. They didn't overcome their separation from God through religious performance. They heard the gospel, believed it, spoke it (magnifying God), and received the Holy Spirit. This same pattern is available to you for every challenge you face.

Bridging the Gap: The Pattern Revealed

The hear-believe-speak-receive pattern isn't something you create. It's how God designed transformation to work. Cornelius and his household heard God's Word about Jesus, believed it, spoke in response, and immediately received the Holy Spirit before Peter even finished preaching. When you position yourself to hear God's truth, transformation proceeds from His Word working in you, not from your effort to make it happen. While Cornelius's story demonstrates salvation, the same pattern applies to every area of life where you need God's grace to transform you.

To Him all the prophets witness that,
through His name,
whoever believes in Him will receive remission of sins.
Acts 10:43

CHAPTER 2:

HEARING THE WORD - THE FOUNDATION OF FAITH

"Faith comes by hearing, and hearing by the word of God" (Romans 10:17). This simple verse reveals the starting point for everything we will be covering from here on out. You cannot believe what you haven't heard, you cannot speak what you don't know, and you cannot receive what you're unaware of. Hearing God's Word is the foundation upon which your entire new creation identity is built.

This principle appears throughout Scripture, including in Paul's letter to the Galatians, where he contrasts two completely different approaches to spiritual life. In Galatians 3:2, Paul asks, *"Did you receive the Spirit by the works of the law, or by the hearing of faith?"* He raises the same question again in verse 5: "Does He who supplies the Spirit to you and works miracles among you do it by the works of the law, or by the hearing of faith?"

Notice the phrase "hearing of faith," not the works of law, not human effort or striving, but hearing that produces faith. This connects directly to what we discovered in Chapter 1 about the Old Covenant versus the New Covenant. The Old Covenant operated through commandments to do, external rules and regulations that demanded performance. The New Covenant operates through words to believe, truth that transforms from the inside out through the hearing of faith.

The Spirit isn't supplied through your works, your discipline, or your religious observance. The Spirit comes, miracles happen, and transformation occurs through hearing God's Word with faith. This is grace in action, God doing for you what you could never accomplish through human effort.

But hearing in the biblical sense is more than casual listening. It's about positioning your heart to receive God's truth, filling your mind with His promises, and creating space for His Word to take root and grow. In our age of endless distractions, this requires deliberateness.

How Faith Comes

Romans 10:17 uses a specific Greek word for "hearing" (*akoe*) that implies receiving and responding to what is heard, not just the physical act of hearing sounds. When the early church gathered, they had to *hear* the Word spoken orally because most people couldn't read, and written copies of Scripture were rare. Believers might have traveled long distances to sit under an apostle's teaching or gather in synagogues to hear the scrolls read aloud.

The early church had to work to hear God's Word. Today, you have it everywhere, but having access isn't the same as hearing. Many believers remain deficient in faith, not because they lack Bibles, but because they're not consistently positioning themselves to hear God's truth work in their hearts. Hearing requires more than availability; it requires attention, intentionality, and regularity.

When I say "weak in faith," I don't mean lacking intelligence or spiritual depth. Faith isn't an intellectual exercise reserved for scholars or theologians. Faith comes to anyone, regardless of education, background, or natural ability, who hears consistently God's Word. A child can have strong faith because they've heard simple truths about Jesus. A highly educated person can have weak faith because they've filled their mind with everything except God's Word.

The weakness in faith that many believers experience stems primarily from a lack of hearing the preaching of God's grace. When you do not hear messages focused primarily on what Christ has done, when teaching emphasizes your performance over His finished work, when the focus stays on behavior reformation rather than identity transformation, faith remains weak because you're not hearing the truth that builds faith, the good news of God's grace.

You can't believe it, speak it, or receive it if you've not heard it. So the goal should always be to hear the word. Hear the word. Hear the word.

Hearing with Purpose

It's helpful to hear God's Word that specifically addresses your situation and needs. If you're battling fear, hear about God's protection and peace. If you're facing financial pressure, hear about His provision. However, not all reading or hearing has to directly reference a specific issue you're experiencing.

In fact, simply beholding Jesus transforms all aspects of our lives. Second Corinthians 3:18 declares, *"But we all, with unveiled face, beholding as in a mirror the glory of the Lord, are being transformed into the same image from glory to glory, just as by the Spirit of the Lord."* This verse reveals a momentous truth: transformation happens through beholding Jesus, not through focusing on your problems or trying to fix yourself.

When you read or hear the Scriptures with the purpose of seeing Jesus, His character, His love, His finished work, His grace, something supernatural occurs. You're not just gaining information about God; you're being transformed by gazing into His face. The Holy Spirit uses the Word to reveal Jesus to your heart, and as you behold Him, you're gradually changed into His likeness.

This means that reading the Gospels to see how Jesus engaged people transforms how you relate to others. Hearing about His compassion toward the broken changes your heart toward those who are hurting. Seeing His patience with struggling disciples gives you patience with yourself and others. Beholding His grace toward sinners dissolves your tendency toward self-righteousness or self-condemnation.

Hearing in Different Seasons

What your spirit needs to hear may vary depending on your life season and circumstances. A new believer might need to focus on foundational truths about salvation and identity in Christ. This includes understanding that righteousness is a gift, not something earned through performance. You are declared righteous the moment you believe in Jesus, not because of what you do, but because of what He has done. Someone facing a health crisis will concentrate on healing Scriptures, storing them in their heart, but always within the context of beholding Jesus as Healer. A person dealing with broken relationships might need to hear about forgiveness and restoration, but ultimately about Jesus as the reconciler and restorer.

Don't feel confined to systematic Bible-reading plans if you're going through a specific trial. It's perfectly appropriate to camp out in passages that speak to your current need while still maintaining the focus on seeing Jesus within those passages. When facing a specific challenge, ask: "How does this Scripture reveal Jesus to me? What aspect of His character, His work, or His grace does this show me?"

The Quick Scripture Reference Guide at the back of this book will help you find relevant passages for specific situations. But remember, even as you turn to these targeted Scriptures, you're not just looking for solutions, you're looking for Jesus, who is the solution.

Quality Matters

Not all Christian content carries the same weight as Scripture itself. While sermons, books, and teachings can be helpful, they're supplements to, not substitutes for, direct intake of God's Word. The Bible itself carries the power to transform (Hebrews 4:12), so make sure you're hearing Scripture, not just commentary about Scripture. Even the best teaching can't replace the living Word speaking directly to your heart.

But here's what happens when you do open Scripture: you often bring Old Covenant thinking into New Covenant promises without realizing it. You read "by His stripes you are healed," but unconsciously add "IF I have enough faith." You read "my God shall supply all your need" but mentally insert "WHEN I'm obedient enough." You read "the truth shall make you free," but think "AFTER I stop sinning." This is mixing law with grace. The promise is based on what Christ accomplished, but you've made it conditional on your performance.

Watch for this pattern in your own thinking: Does this promise depend on what Jesus did or what I must do? When you read about healing, provision, freedom, or peace, do you immediately start calculating whether you're good enough, faithful enough, or obedient enough to receive it? That's law creeping into grace. The New Covenant isn't "Jesus did His part, now I do mine." It's "Jesus finished the work, now I receive by faith." If you're filling your mind with content that emphasizes your performance over Christ's finished work, or that mixes grace promises with law-based conditions, those inputs will compete with God's truth for influence in your heart.

This is why direct engagement with Scripture matters so profoundly. When you read God's Word yourself, asking the Holy Spirit to illuminate it, you can catch yourself adding conditions that aren't there. You can recognize when you're shifting from "because of what Christ did" to "because of what I must do." The goal is to hear God's Word purely, without the filter of merit-driven thinking that the Old Covenant trained us to have. Let Scripture speak grace. Don't let your mind add law.

Hearing with Expectation

Approach God's Word expecting it to show you Jesus and, through that revelation, speak to your situation. The same Holy Spirit who inspired Scripture lives within you and can illuminate its meaning for your life. Come with the attitude that God wants to speak to you through His Word.

This expectation makes all the difference in how you hear. Instead of passively reading or listening, you're actively looking for how Jesus is revealed in the passage. You're asking: "What does this show me about His character? How does this reveal His love? What does this teach me about His finished work?" As you behold Him in Scripture, transformation follows naturally.

Consider what happened on the road to Emmaus in Luke 24. Two discouraged disciples were walking away from Jerusalem, devastated by Jesus's crucifixion. Their hopes had been crushed. Everything they'd believed seemed to have ended in failure. Then Jesus Himself joined them on the road, though they didn't recognize Him. He asked what they were discussing, and they poured out their grief and confusion.

Jesus's response is remarkable: *"And beginning at Moses and all the Prophets, He expounded to them in all the Scriptures the things concerning Himself" (Luke 24:27).* He didn't give them a pep talk or rebuke their lack of faith. Instead, He opened the Scriptures and showed them how everything pointed to Him; His suffering, His glory, His purpose. Later, after they recognized Him and He vanished from their sight, they said to each other, *"Did not our heart burn within us while He talked with us on the road, and while He opened the Scriptures to us?" (Luke 24:32).*

This is a hearing with expectation. When you approach Scripture looking for Jesus, your heart will burn within you just as theirs did. The Holy Spirit will illuminate Christ in passages you've read dozens of times before. You'll see Him in the sacrificial system of Leviticus, in the prophecies of Isaiah, in the poetry of the Psalms. The entire Bible, from Genesis to Revelation, reveals Jesus. And as He's revealed to you through Scripture, something supernatural happens in your heart. Faith rises. Hope is restored. Transformation begins. This is why hearing God's Word with the expectation of seeing Jesus is so powerful. He's there on every page, waiting to reveal Himself to you.

The Goal of Hearing

Remember, the ultimate goal isn't just to acquire biblical knowledge or even to find answers to specific problems. The goal is to behold Jesus, to see Him more clearly, know Him more deeply, and be transformed by His glory revealed in Scripture. As 2 Corinthians 3:18 promises, when you gaze at Him with an unveiled face, you're transformed into His image from glory to glory by the Spirit.

What does it mean to behold Christ with "unveiled face"? In 2 Corinthians 3:14-16, Paul explains that when people read the Old Testament without Christ, *"a veil lies over their hearts."* But *"when one turns to the Lord, the veil* is removed." Then in verse 18, Paul declares that we who believe "all, with unveiled face, beholding as in a mirror the glory of the Lord, are being transformed into the same image." The unveiled face, then, is the face of Christ revealed throughout all of Scripture. When you turn to Jesus in faith, the veil is lifted, and suddenly the entire Bible—from Genesis to Revelation—becomes a revelation of Him.

Consider Joseph's story in Genesis. With unveiled face, you now see what was always there: Joseph, the beloved son of his father, specially favored and given a coat signifying his unique position. His brothers rejected him out of jealousy and sold him for pieces of silver. He was falsely accused and suffered wrongfully, descending into the pit and then into prison. Yet God raised him to the right hand of Pharaoh's power, where he alone had authority to distribute bread and save the whole nation from death. Everyone had to come through Joseph to receive what they needed to live. Do you see Him? This is Jesus: the Father's beloved Son, rejected by His own, sold for silver, falsely accused, who descended into death but was raised to the right hand of all power and authority. Now He alone distributes the bread of life, and anyone who comes to Him will never hunger.

This is beholding with unveiled face; seeing Jesus revealed throughout Scripture. The veil is gone. Christ appears on every page. Every promise, every type, every prophecy points to Him. And as you behold Him revealed in all of God's Word, something supernatural happens: you're transformed into His image. Not by trying to be like Joseph or any other biblical hero, not by following principles extracted from their stories, but simply by seeing Jesus more clearly. The transformation flows from beholding Him, from seeing His character, His love, His finished work displayed throughout the entire Bible from beginning to end.

You're hearing so you can believe, speak, and receive. Each time you expose yourself to Scripture, looking for Jesus, you're creating an opportunity for faith to grow and for God's promises to become reality in your life. But more than that, you're being changed into His likeness simply by beholding Him with an unveiled face.

The pattern always begins here: hear the Word with the purpose of seeing Jesus. Make it a priority, make it purposeful, and make it fresh. Everything else in your journey as a new creation flows from this foundation of beholding Christ in Scripture.

Just as you need fresh food daily, you need a fresh intake of God's Word. Yesterday's reading was important, but today brings new challenges that require current input from Scripture. When you approach Scripture daily looking for Jesus, you're not just reviewing what you already know; you're encountering Him fresh each day. The Holy Spirit makes the Word alive and relevant for today's specific needs as you behold Christ within its pages.

Bridging the Gap: Hearing the Word – The Foundation of Faith

Faith doesn't come from trying harder or being more sincere. It comes from hearing God's Word. Romans 10:17 reveals that repeated exposure to Scripture naturally builds faith, not through human effort but through the divine power of the Word itself. The more you hear about your righteousness in Christ, the more naturally you'll live from it, because God's Word does the transforming work as you position yourself to receive it.

So then faith comes by hearing,
and hearing by the word of God.

Romans 10:17

CHAPTER 3:

FAITH IGNITED - FROM HEARING TO BELIEVING

In Chapter 1, we saw how Cornelius and his household experienced transformation through a simple but powerful pattern: they heard Peter preach the gospel, believed the message in their hearts, spoke in tongues, magnifying God, and received the Holy Spirit. The pattern was complete and immediate: hear, believe, speak, and receive. Cornelius approached that moment with eager expectation—an angel had spoken! He knew something good was coming. That expectancy matters as you move from hearing to believing. Let's explore what it means to position yourself to receive.

Expectancy: Position to Receive

For the past few days, I've been checking my front porch multiple times a day. I ordered new Gym Shark workout pants, and I knew they were on the way. Every time I walked past the door, I'd glance out—not because I was anxious, but because I was expecting something good. That's a completely different mindset than the random times I happen to walk past the door when I'm not expecting anything. Same door, same porch, but my expectancy changed how I approached it. When you come to God's Word with expectancy, you're positioning yourself the same way: ready to receive what you know is coming.

When you pick up your Bible with expectancy, you're saying: "God, I'm here. I'm listening. I believe You have something for me in these pages today." You might not know if it'll be comfort, correction, revelation about your identity, or faith for a specific situation—but you're confident something good is coming because that's who God is.

This isn't wishful thinking or manufactured emotion; it's based on God's character and promises. Hebrews 11:6 makes this clear: God *"is a rewarder of those who diligently seek Him."* Let that sink in. God actively rewards seeking. When you come to His Word, you're not hoping He might notice or wondering if He'll show up—He's already committed to rewarding your pursuit of Him. The word *"rewarder"* isn't passive; it describes someone who takes pleasure in giving to those who seek Him. You're not twisting God's arm or trying to earn something through spiritual discipline. You're coming to a generous Father who loves to reveal Himself to hungry hearts.

What does He reward you with? Faith. Understanding. Peace. Direction. Revelation of who He is and who you are in Him. Sometimes it's a specific verse that addresses exactly what you're facing. Sometimes it's a broader truth about His character that strengthens your foundation. But He rewards seeking, so can expect to receive when you come to His Word.

James 1:5 reinforces this: God *"gives to all liberally and without reproach."* He's not stingy with His truth. He doesn't hold back or make you beg. The word *"liberally"* means generously, abundantly, without reservation. And *"without reproach"* means He doesn't scold you for coming or make you feel guilty for needing to hear from Him again. You can approach His Word with confidence that He wants to give you what you need.

The psalmist understood this when he declared, *"My soul, wait silently for God alone, for my expectation is from Him"* (Psalm 62:5). Your expectation isn't in the act of reading itself, but in God speaking to you through what you read. You're not depending on your ability to extract meaning or your skill at Bible study. You're depending on God's faithfulness to reveal Himself to those who seek Him.

So you open the Bible expecting to receive, not just hoping you might stumble across something helpful. That expectancy changes everything. It's the difference between hearing words and hearing God's Word—between information passing through your mind and truth taking root in your heart.

When Belief Becomes Difficult

But what happens when believing becomes difficult, or when hearing doesn't lead to believing? When you've heard God's Word clearly, you want to believe it, yet something inside struggles to fully embrace it. This is where many believers find themselves stuck, knowing what God says but wrestling with doubts born from years of disappointment, unanswered prayers, or circumstances that seem to contradict His promises.

The second step in our pattern, believing, is often the most challenging, especially when you've been dealing with a situation for years with no apparent change. Yet this is also where we discover the depths of God's grace, because He doesn't require perfect faith before He acts. He honors honest faith, even when it's mixed with doubt.

The story in Mark 9:17-27 captures this struggle perfectly and shows us how Jesus responds to honest faith mixed with doubt. Let's set the scene carefully, because the context reveals why belief was so difficult for this desperate father.

A crowd had gathered around Jesus's disciples, who were arguing with the scribes. When Jesus arrived and asked what the commotion was about, a man from the crowd called out, "Teacher, I brought You my son, who has a mute spirit. And wherever it seizes him, it throws him down; he foams at the mouth, gnashes his teeth, and becomes rigid. So I spoke to Your disciples, that they should cast it out, but they could not."

Picture the father's desperation. His son had been tormented since childhood, thrown into fire and water by this demonic spirit, convulsing violently, unable to speak, suffering terribly. The father had watched helplessly as his child experienced seizures so severe that bystanders thought the boy was dead. This was every parent's worst nightmare, repeated year after year.

He had tried everything. Home remedies passed down through generations. Visits to physicians who had no answers. Prayers at the synagogue seemed to echo into empty silence. He'd probably made vows to God, bargained with heaven, and wept countless tears. Nothing worked. Nothing changed. Year after year, his son suffered while he stood by, powerless to help.

Then he heard about Jesus's disciples having the authority to cast out demons. Hope flickered again, maybe this time would be different. He brought his son to the disciples, believing they could help. But after they prayed and commanded the demon to leave, nothing happened. The demon remained. His son continued suffering. Another failure. Another disappointment. Another prayer that seemed to go unanswered.

Perhaps you know this feeling. You've prayed about something for years, a health condition, a financial crisis, a broken relationship, a prodigal child. You've believed God's promises, stood on His Word, and declared His truth. Yet the situation hasn't changed. If anything, it's gotten worse. Each failed attempt to see a breakthrough has eroded your confidence, making it harder to believe the next time you hear God's promises.

Maybe you've even experienced what this father did, other believers trying to help but unable to produce the breakthrough you need. Well-meaning Christians have prayed over you, prophesied over you, laid hands on you, but you walked away still carrying the same burden. The cumulative burden of disappointment makes it increasingly difficult to believe that this time will be different.

This is the context in which Jesus spoke to the father: "If you can believe, all things are possible to him who believes." On the surface, it sounds like Jesus was placing the entire burden on the father's ability to generate enough faith. But what happened next reveals something far more gracious.

Jesus Honors Honest Struggle

The father's response is one of the most honest cries in all of Scripture: "Lord, I believe; help my unbelief!" He wasn't pretending to have faith he didn't possess. He wasn't trying to manufacture confidence he didn't feel. He was simply being honest about the tension in his heart. He wanted to believe, he chose to believe, but years of disappointment made full confidence difficult.

Here's something crucial to understand: doubt is not the same as unbelief. Doubt, "I'm not certain this will work, but I'm willing to trust God anyway." Unbelief says, "God's Word isn't true, and I won't act on it." The father had uncertainty but not unbelief. He brought his son to Jesus despite years of disappointment. He admitted his struggle but didn't walk away. That's faith, imperfect, struggling, honest faith, but faith nonetheless. That father is saying, *"I believe, but I need help with my lack of confidence. I believe, but I struggle with full assurance. I have faith, but it's not yet strong."*

Jesus didn't rebuke the father for his doubt. He didn't give him a lecture on having stronger faith or tell him to try harder to believe. Instead, He immediately cast out the demon and healed the boy. Jesus honored the father's honest struggle and met him with grace.

This reveals something profound about belief in the New Covenant: even when you have full belief, even when you're standing firmly on God's promises, there's still a complete dependence on Jesus to perform and provide. You're not trusting in the strength of your faith; you're trusting in the faithfulness of God. The father believed that Jesus could heal his son, but he recognized that the actual healing depended entirely on Jesus's power and willingness, not on the perfection of his own faith.

This is liberating. You don't have to generate perfect faith before God acts. You don't have to eliminate every doubt before He moves. You simply have to bring what faith you have to Jesus and depend on Him to do what only He can do. Your healing doesn't depend on perfect belief; it depends on His perfect faithfulness. Your provision doesn't come from flawless faith; it comes from His abundant grace. Your breakthrough doesn't require doubt-free confidence; it requires bringing your struggling faith to the One who is faithful.

Grace to Believe

The father's cry, "Help my unbelief!" was actually a profound prayer for grace. He was essentially saying, "Jesus, I'm bringing You my faith, but I recognize it's not enough on its own. I need Your help even to believe what You're capable of doing. Give me the grace to trust You fully."

And Jesus gave it to him.

This is New Covenant grace in action, revealing a dimension of God's goodness that many believers have never grasped. Under the Old Covenant, you had to muster up faith on your own through human effort and willpower. Gideon needed multiple signs with his fleece. The ten spies could not generate enough faith to enter the Promised Land, and an entire generation suffered for their inability to produce faith. Even righteous Zechariah was struck mute when he struggled to believe the angel's promise. If you couldn't believe strongly enough, you simply failed, and there was no grace to bridge the gap.

But now, under the New Covenant, even faith itself is recognized as a gift (Ephesians 2:8). When you struggle to believe God's Word, you can pray for grace to believe it, and God will provide that grace.

Think about what this means for your daily struggles. When you're standing on Isaiah 53:5, "By His stripes we are healed," but still feel sick, and symptoms persist, you can pray: *"Lord, I believe Your Word about healing; help my unbelief. Give me grace to trust You despite what I feel in my body."* When you're trusting Philippians 4:19, "My God shall supply all my need," while facing financial pressure, you can declare: "Father, I believe Your promise about provision; help my unbelief. Grant me grace to rest in Your faithfulness despite my circumstances."

This prayer has become a lifeline for countless believers facing seasons when God's promises seemed distant from their reality. Instead of feeling condemned for doubt or pressured to manufacture stronger faith through sheer willpower, they've found freedom in admitting their struggle and asking for help. And Jesus always provides the grace to keep believing until His Word becomes reality in their circumstances. The grace to believe isn't something you generate; it's something you receive from the One who is the author and finisher of your faith.

The Process of Believing

Belief isn't usually a one-time event; it's often a process, and that process involves cycling back through the very beginning of the pattern: hearing God's Word again. You hear a promise, choose to believe it, but then circumstances or past experiences challenge that belief. This is when you don't give up or condemn yourself; you simply return to hearing.

Go back to the Scripture you're standing on and hear it again. Read it aloud. Listen to it being preached. Meditate on it until it fills your heart once more. Ask for grace to believe, and keep declaring God's truth over your situation. This cycling back to hearing is not a sign of weak faith; it's the practical outworking of how faith grows and matures.

This is what Romans 4:20 means when it says Abraham "was strengthened in faith." The Greek word implies a continuous, repeated process; he kept being strengthened. It wasn't a one-time boost but an ongoing reinforcement. Every time doubt arose, or circumstances seemed impossible, Abraham returned to God's promise about having descendants as numerous as the stars. He heard it again in his spirit, chose to believe it again, and was strengthened again.

Here's something vital to understand: belief is ultimately a choice, not a feeling. The father in Mark 9 chose to believe despite his feelings of doubt. He chose to bring his son to Jesus despite years of disappointment. He chose to ask for help rather than walk away in despair. And God honored that choice with grace, sustaining his faith until the breakthrough came.

In difficult situations, your choice to believe is honored by God with His grace to believe. You're not generating faith through positive thinking or emotional manipulation; you're making a deliberate decision to trust God's Word over your circumstances, and He provides the grace to maintain that trust. The father of the demon-possessed boy chose to believe despite years of watching his son suffer with no relief. His past experiences could have justified unbelief, but he chose to trust Jesus anyway, and that choice opened the door for God's grace to flow.

Consider how this works with anxiety. When worry overwhelms you, cycle back to hearing Isaiah 26:3

"You will keep him in perfect peace, whose mind is stayed on You, because he trusts in You."

Anxiety tells you that everything is falling apart, that you can't handle what's coming, that the future is terrifying. But you choose to hear God's Word again. You speak it aloud: "God keeps me in perfect peace because my mind is stayed on Him." Then you ask: "Lord, I choose to believe Your promise of peace; help my unbelief. Give me grace to trust You despite this anxiety." Each time worry resurfaces, you return to hearing that verse, choose to believe it again, and God strengthens your faith through the cycle.

Or perhaps you're battling guilt over past failures. Condemnation keeps replaying your mistakes, telling you God couldn't possibly accept you after what you've done. That's when you cycle back to hearing Romans 5:1

"Therefore, having been justified by faith, we have peace with God through our Lord Jesus Christ."

Guilt says you're disqualified, but God's Word says you're justified, declared righteous through faith in Christ. You make the choice: "I choose to believe I have peace with God through Jesus." You pray: "Lord, I believe I'm justified by faith; help my unbelief. Give me grace to accept Your acceptance of me." Each time guilt tries to condemn you, return to hearing that Scripture, choose to believe it again, and let God's grace silence the accusations.

This continuous cycling through the hear-believe-speak-receive pattern isn't a sign that something's wrong with your faith; it's how faith matures and grows stronger. Each time you return to hearing, choose to believe again, speak God's truth, and depend on Him to provide, you're being strengthened just as Abraham was. The process itself is part of God's grace, gradually shaping your heart to trust Him more fully.

Bridging the Gap: Faith Ignited - From Hearing to Believing

Believing isn't just mental agreement. It's choosing to trust God's truth over what you see, feel, or experience. The father in Mark 9 cried out, "Lord, I believe; help my unbelief!" showing that belief is a choice you make, even when doubts remain, and the Father is gracious when you choose to believe. True faith looks away from yourself and your limitations to focus entirely on God's ability and willingness to perform what He's promised.

"Lord, I believe; help my unbelief!"

Mark 9:24

CHAPTER 4:

SPEAKING LIFE OR DEATH - THE POWER OF YOUR WORDS

"Death and life are in the power of the tongue, and those who love it will eat its fruit" (Proverbs 18:21). Your words carry more power than you might realize. They don't just describe your reality, they help shape it. This is why the third step in our pattern, speaking God's Word, is so crucial for walking in your new creation identity.

The tongue is the bridge between what you believe in your heart and what you receive in your life. As Jesus said, *"Out of the abundance of the heart the mouth speaks"* (Luke 6:45). What fills your heart will eventually come out of your mouth, and what comes out of your mouth will influence what you experience in life.

Two Voices, Two Choices

Every day you face a choice between two voices: the voice of the old man and the voice of the new creation. The old man speaks from past experience, current circumstances, and natural limitations. The new creation speaks from God's Word, eternal promises, and supernatural possibilities.

The Old Man Says: "I can't overcome this addiction." "My marriage is hopeless." "I'll never get out of debt." "This sickness will kill me." "I'm not good enough."

The New Creation says, "I can do all things through Christ who strengthens me." "God is able to restore what's been broken." "My God supplies all my needs according to His riches." "By His stripes I am healed." "I am the righteousness of God in Christ."

Now, before you think I'm suggesting you walk around your house talking to yourself like a crazy person, let me be clear: you're already talking to yourself all day long. The question is whether you're agreeing with the old man's obituary or the new creation's birth certificate.

It's remarkably easy to default to the old way of thinking and speaking. Your natural senses, your past experiences, and the voices around you all collude to pull you back into the familiar patterns of the old man. When you look at your bank account, the old voice screams. When you feel pain in your body, the old voice declares defeat. When relationships strain, the old voice replays every failure and disappointment. This is the path of least resistance, the well-worn groove your mind naturally falls into without conscious effort.

Even recently, I have caught myself saying simple, even subconscious phrases, like "I'm so busy right now." "I'm stressed." "I don't feel good." "I feel awful." "I'm nervous." "That concerns me." And on and on… To be honest, I did have a lot on my plate, and I had flu-like symptoms for 10 days just this past Christmas. These are real conditions to contend with, and even I found the wrong words slipping out just out of pure habit. You must be deliberate with the words you allow to leave your mouth.

Speaking as the new creation, though it may feel unnatural at first, carries a profound affirmation that settles deep in your spirit. When you declare "I am the righteousness of God in Christ" despite feelings of unworthiness, something shifts inside you. When you speak "By His stripes I am healed" while symptoms persist, faith rises to meet God's promise. These aren't empty words or positive thinking; they're declarations of what God has already said is true about you, and they are aligning your words, and therefore the direction of your faith, to the truth of God's Word.

Each time you choose to speak from your new creation identity rather than your circumstances, you're aligning yourself with heaven's reality and positioning yourself to receive what grace has already provided. The more you speak this way, the more natural it becomes, until the voice of the new creation becomes your default response rather than the exception.

My husband and I had once experienced a season of stress, anxiety, and doubt, looking intently for a change in circumstances that would certainly improve our situation. In the interim, however, the heaviness of anxiety, and quite frankly fear, was more than we had experienced before. We were really struggling. My husband then made a suggestion: *"Let's play a game. Let's see how many bible passages we can think of off the top of our heads. I'll go first."* Not being real bible scholars, you can probably guess the game didn't last all afternoon. But what happened was absolutely remarkable: the mood shifted. The air was lighter, and that heaviness began to dissipate.

Our focus was shifted from our problems to His promises. We were encouraged in our hearts and reminded that He loved us and cared for us. This gave us the strength to let the fears go.

And this is the key moment in the application of our hear-believe-speak-receive pattern. Our situation hadn't changed. And certainly, the doubts would creep back in the next day. But we found a strategy that gave us the day's victory and even made us stronger for the fight tomorrow.

The voice you choose to express determines which reality you'll experience.

Jesus' Example

Jesus demonstrated the power of speaking God's truth. When He faced the devil's temptations in the wilderness, He didn't argue or explain; He simply spoke Scripture: "It is written..." (Matthew 4:4, 7, 10). This phrase is profoundly significant; it reveals that the words we speak must be grounded in Scripture, not in worldly wisdom or our natural senses.

Notice that Jesus didn't say, "I feel," or "I think," or "In my experience." He didn't draw on human philosophy or natural reasoning. He anchored every response in what God had already declared in His Word: "It is written." This wasn't just a convenient debating technique; it was a demonstration of the only foundation strong enough to resist the enemy's attacks. Worldly wisdom shifts with changing circumstances. Natural senses report only what they perceive in the moment. But God's written Word stands forever, unchanging and unshakeable.

When you speak based on what you see, feel, or think, you're building on sand that shifts with every wave of circumstance. But when you speak "It is written," you're standing on the eternal rock of God's truth. The devil can argue with your feelings, dispute your reasoning, and challenge your experiences. But he cannot overturn what God has written. This is why your words must flow from Scripture rather than from natural observation or human wisdom.

Second Corinthians 4:8-13 gives us another powerful glimpse into this principle: "We are hard-pressed on every side, yet not crushed; we are perplexed, but not in despair; persecuted, but not forsaken; struck down, but not destroyed." Notice Paul's honest acknowledgment of difficulty; he doesn't pretend the pressure isn't real or that the perplexity doesn't exist. But he refuses to let natural circumstances have the final word.

The passage continues with the key to this victory: "Since we have the same spirit of faith, according to what is written, 'I believed, and therefore I spoke,' we also believe and therefore speak." Here it is again, "according to what is written." Paul's speaking wasn't rooted in denying his circumstances but in declaring God's truth over those circumstances. He believed what God said, and therefore he spoke it. Not because everything felt good or looked promising, but because God's Word is more real than anything our senses can perceive.

This is the pattern for every believer: believe what is written, then speak what you believe. Your words carry authority when they're anchored in Scripture rather than in the shifting sands of feelings, opinions, or natural observation.

When He calmed the storm, He spoke to it directly: "Peace, be still!" (Mark 4:39). When He raised Lazarus, He declared, "Lazarus, come forth!" (John 11:43). Jesus' words carried the authority of heaven because they aligned with the Father's will and were grounded in eternal truth, not temporary circumstances.

Speaking vs. Confessing: Out of the Abundance of the Heart

There's an important distinction between merely talking and actually confessing God's Word. *Confession* means "to say the same thing," agreeing with what God has already said about your situation. But here's what many believers miss: effective confession flows from a heart filled with God's Word, not from sheer willpower or religious duty.

Remember what Jesus said in Luke 6:45: "Out of the abundance of the heart the mouth speaks." This reveals a crucial truth about speaking God's Word. When your heart is full of Scripture through diligent hearing, confession becomes a natural overflow rather than a forced effort. The words flow from the inside out, not because you're trying hard to say the right things, but because you can't help but speak what fills your heart.

This is why the hear-believe-speak-receive pattern always begins with hearing. If you skip the hearing part and jump straight to speaking, confession becomes grueling effort. You're constantly trying to remember what you're supposed to say, forcing words that don't feel genuine, and straining to maintain declarations that have no root in your heart. It's like trying to draw water from an empty well.

But when you've consistently heard God's Word, when it has taken root in your heart, and you've come to believe it, speaking becomes the natural expression of what's already inside you. The confession isn't manufactured through effort; it bubbles up from the abundance in your heart.

Consider the difference:

Talking is giving your opinion or describing your circumstances based on what you see and feel: "I feel so sick today," "This situation is impossible," "Nothing ever works out for me," "I'm so worried about these bills."

Confessing is declaring what God says, regardless of circumstances, flowing from a heart that has received His truth: "By His stripes I am healed," "With God all things are possible," "All things work together for my good," "My God supplies all my needs according to His riches in glory."

Confession isn't denying reality; it's declaring a higher reality. When you say "By His stripes I am healed" while still experiencing symptoms, you're not pretending the symptoms don't exist. You're declaring that God's Word is more real than what you feel. But this declaration only carries power and feels authentic when it flows from a heart that has heard and believed Isaiah 53:5.

Here's the practical application: When facing financial pressure, instead of immediately trying to force yourself to speak prosperity scriptures, first spend time hearing God's Word about His provision. Read Matthew 6:25-34 slowly. Listen to Philippians 4:19. Meditate on 2 Corinthians 9:8. Let these truths sink into your heart through repetition and meditation. As you hear them again and again, belief begins to form. And as belief takes root, confession becomes the natural overflow.

When dealing with sickness, rather than robotically repeating "I am healed" out of obligation, saturate your heart with healing scriptures. Hear Isaiah 53:4-5 until it becomes more real to you than your symptoms. Listen to Psalm 103:2-3 until your spirit resonates with God's promise. When your heart is full of these truths, speaking them becomes as natural as breathing.

When struggling with fear, don't just try to talk yourself into courage. Fill your heart with 2 Timothy 1:7, Isaiah 41:10, and Psalm 23 through consistent hearing. When these truths saturate your inner world, speaking "God has not given me a spirit of fear" isn't a forced exercise; it's the authentic expression of what you truly believe.

The abundance of the heart determines the words of the mouth. This means your primary focus should always be on hearing God's Word until your heart is so full that speaking it becomes inevitable. When confession flows from the abundance of a Word-filled heart, it carries genuine faith rather than empty repetition. You're not trying to convince yourself of something you don't really believe; you're simply declaring what has already become real to you through hearing and believing God's truth.

Preaching to Yourself and Your Family

One of the most important uses of your tongue is preaching to yourself. David did this throughout the Psalms, commanding his soul to trust God and remember His benefits. You need to regularly remind yourself of who you are in Christ and what God has promised you.

Declare your identity in Christ: *"I am a new creation in Christ," "I am more than a conqueror," "I am righteous through His gift."*

But this principle extends beyond just speaking to yourself. Speaking God's Word over your family, especially your children, is one of the most powerful ways to establish faith in your home. Children's hearts are remarkably responsive to hearing Scripture, and when they consistently hear the truth about what Christ has done for them, faith naturally takes root.

Often, the most effective approach is to speak scriptures without lengthy commentary or explanation. Simply stating *"He Himself bore our sickness"* over a sick child, or declaring *"God supplies all our needs according to His riches in glory"* when the family faces financial challenges, plants seeds of faith that the Holy Spirit waters and brings to fruition. Your children don't need you to explain or defend God's promises; they need to hear them spoken with confidence and authority.

When your daughter is anxious about a test, speak Philippians 4:6-7 over her: *"Be anxious for nothing, but in everything by prayer and supplication, with thanksgiving, let your requests be made known to God; and the peace of God, which surpasses all understanding, will guard your hearts and minds through Christ Jesus."* When your son faces rejection or disappointment, remind him with Ephesians 1:6 that he is *"accepted in the Beloved."*

This isn't about creating a religious ritual or turning every moment into a teaching opportunity. It's about naturally filling your home with the sound of God's Word so that your children grow up hearing the wonderful works Christ has already accomplished for them. When they hear you speaking Scripture over circumstances, they learn by example that God's Word is the foundation for life, not just theory to be studied but truth to be lived.

Guarding Your Words

Just as important as speaking life is avoiding words of death. Watch for these destructive speech patterns:

Complaining and murmuring, speaking defeat over your family, agreeing with the enemy's lies, rehearsing past failures, declaring impossibility over God's promises.

When you catch yourself speaking contrary to God's Word, stop and redirect. Replace the negative confession with truth from Scripture.

David provides a powerful example of how to guard your words even while being honest about difficulties. Throughout the Psalms, he frequently recounts his trials, acknowledges his pain, and describes his circumstances with raw honesty. He doesn't pretend everything is fine when it isn't. But notice what he always does: he refuses to let the problem have the final word.

In Psalm 13, David cries out, "How long, O Lord? Will You forget me forever? How long will You hide Your face from me? How long shall I take counsel in my soul, having sorrow in my heart daily?" He's honest about his pain and confusion. But he doesn't end there. He turns: "But I have trusted in Your mercy; my heart shall rejoice in Your salvation. I will sing to the Lord, because He has dealt bountifully with me."

You see this pattern repeated throughout the Psalms. Psalm 42 begins with "Why are you cast down, O my soul? And why are you disquieted within me?" acknowledging real distress. But it continues: "Hope in God, for I shall yet praise Him for the help of His countenance." Psalm 73 describes the writer's near-fatal stumbling when he envied the wicked, but concludes: "Nevertheless I am continually with You; You hold me by my right hand."

The phrase "but God" appears again and again in Scripture as a turning point between circumstance and truth, between what we see and what God says. David felt forgotten, but God was still his salvation. He was cast down, but God was still worthy of hope and praise. The circumstances were real, but God's truth was more real.

This is the pattern for guarding your words: Acknowledge what you're facing without letting those circumstances define your reality. You can be honest about the pressure without speaking defeat. The key is always to turn from the problem to the promise, from what you see to what God says, from the temporary to the eternal. Let your words acknowledge the battle, but always give God the final word.

The Holy Spirit is your helper in this journey of speaking God's Word. Jesus promised in John 14:26 that "the Helper, the Holy Spirit, whom the Father will send in My name, He will teach you all things, and bring to your remembrance all things that I said to you." You don't have to strain to remember the right scriptures for every situation.

As you fill your heart with God's Word through consistent hearing, the Holy Spirit will bring those scriptures to your remembrance exactly when you need them. In moments of fear, He'll remind you of God's promises of peace. When facing a lack, He'll bring to mind scriptures about provision. When sickness attacks, He'll quicken healing verses to your heart.

Invite the Holy Spirit to guide you into all truth and remind you of Christ's words. When challenging situations arise, don't panic trying to remember what you're supposed to say. Instead, pause and ask: "Holy Spirit, what does Your Word say about this? Remind me of the higher reality found in Scripture." Then listen for what He brings to your mind and speak it with confidence.

You might be surprised how specific scriptures you've heard suddenly come alive in your memory at the exact moment you need them. This is the Holy Spirit doing what Jesus promised, bringing God's Word to your remembrance and leading you into truth. Trust Him to be your helper in this process of learning to speak life rather than death.

Bridging the Gap: Speaking Life or Death – The Power of Your Words

Your words don't create reality, but they reveal what you truly believe and cooperate with either faith or fear. When you speak God's truth over your circumstances—not denying reality but declaring a higher reality—your words align with His Word and position you to receive what He's already provided. Death and life are in the power of the tongue; you're either speaking agreement with God's promises or with the enemy's lies.

*"Death and life are in the power of the tongue,
and those who love it will eat its fruit."*

Proverbs 18:21

CHAPTER 5:

RECEIVING THROUGH GRACE - THE WORD DOES THE WORK

The final step in our pattern, receiving, is often the most misunderstood. Many believers think receiving God's promises requires intense effort, perfect faith, or flawless performance. But the New Covenant reveals a stunning truth: you don't make God's Word work; it works in you.

"When you received the word of God which you heard from us, you welcomed it not as the word of men, but as it is in truth, the word of God, which also effectively works in you who believe."

1 Thessalonians 2:13

This is crucial to understand: this book isn't a self-help guide with seven steps to a better you. It's not another program to master or a method to perfect through your discipline and determination. What we're revealing here is far more powerful than any human system; it's the Word of God itself doing the transforming work in you. Your role isn't to make transformation happen through effort and striving. Your role is to position yourself to hear God's Word, believe it, speak it, and then allow it to do its work.

The emphasis is on "allow." You're not forcing change, manufacturing spiritual growth, or working up enough faith to see results. You're simply creating space for God's living Word to accomplish what it was sent to do. Like a seed planted in good soil, the Word contains within itself everything necessary for growth and fruit. The seed doesn't need your help to become a plant; it just needs the right environment. Similarly, God's Word doesn't need your self-effort to transform you; it needs your faith-filled reception and your willingness to let it work.

The Word Is Alive and Active

Hebrews 4:12 reveals the fundamental reason why this process works: "For the Word of God is living and powerful, and sharper than any two-edged sword, piercing even to the division of soul and spirit, and of joints and marrow, and is a discerner of the thoughts and intents of the heart."

Notice the present-tense description: the Word of God IS living. Not was living when it was first written, not will be living someday in the future, but IS living right now. This means the Bible you hold in your hands, the scripture you hear preached, the verse you meditate on, carries within it the active, dynamic life of God Himself. It's not merely ancient wisdom or moral instruction; it's the living breath of God that continues to speak, move, and work in everyone who receives it.

The Word is also powerful. The Greek word used here is "energes," from which we get our English word "energy." God's Word is energized, activated, and filled with divine power to accomplish what it was sent to do. When you receive a scripture about healing, you're not just receiving information about God's healing power; you're receiving the healing power itself contained within that Word. When you hear a promise about provision, you're not just learning a theological concept; you're accessing the provision that flows through that promise.

This same truth appears in 1 Thessalonians 2:13, which tells us that God's Word "effectively works in you who believe." The word for "effectively works" is energeo, that same Greek root. God's Word energizes, activates, and produces results in those who believe it. This isn't passive information sitting inert on a page; it's active power at work within you, accomplishing a transformation you could never achieve through human effort.

And notice what this living, powerful Word does: it pierces. It doesn't just sit on the surface of your life, making suggestions. It cuts deep, penetrating to the division of soul and spirit, distinguishing between what belongs to your old nature and what belongs to your new creation identity. Like a spiritual surgeon, God's Word goes to work inside you, cutting away lies and building truth, destroying strongholds of wrong thinking and establishing God's reality in your heart.

Think about this: when a doctor prescribes medicine, you don't take the pill and then try to heal yourself. You simply swallow the medicine and allow it to do what it was designed to do in your body. You might not feel it working immediately, you might not understand the biochemical processes taking place, but you trust that the medicine contains the power to heal, and you let it work. God's Word functions the same way. You don't have to understand all the mechanisms of how it transforms you. You simply receive it by faith and allow it to do its work.

True Repentance: Changing Your Mind About God

For years, many believers have been taught that repentance means feeling sorry for sin, turning from bad behavior, or proving you're serious about change through works. This performance-based understanding of repentance has left countless Christians trapped in cycles of guilt and striving, constantly examining their behavior to see if they've "repented enough." But there's a freedom in Scripture's actual definition that changes everything.

The Greek word for repentance is "*metanoia,*" which literally means "to change your mind" or "to have a different perspective." True biblical repentance isn't primarily about your behavior. It's about changing your mind about who God is. Consider the lost sheep in Luke 15. That sheep didn't do anything to earn rescue. It didn't feel remorseful or promise to do better. It simply encountered the shepherd's pursuing love, was lifted onto his shoulders, and carried home. When Jesus explained this parable, He called it repentance: "I say to you that likewise there will be more joy in heaven over one sinner who repents" (Luke 15:7). The sheep did nothing. Repentance occurred when it encountered the shepherd's relentless love.

Look at the Cornelius story in Acts 10-11. When Peter recounted what happened to the Jerusalem believers, they declared, "Then God has also granted to the Gentiles repentance to life" (Acts 11:18). But what did Cornelius and his household actually do? They heard the gospel, believed it, and received the Holy Spirit. There was no behavior modification, no turning from specific sins, no probationary period. Their "repentance" was simply believing the good news about Jesus. They changed their minds about who God is and what He'd done for them.

This is the repentance Romans 2:4 describes: "The goodness of God leads you to repentance." Not His anger. Not His threats. Not His disappointment. His goodness: His kindness, His grace, His unconditional love. When you truly see God's character through His Word, your mind changes. Notice what produces repentance: it's not your regret over past failures, not your remorse about sin, not your renewed commitment to try harder. It's encountering the goodness of God. For years, you may have thought He was angry with you, that you had to perform to earn His favor, that His blessings came only after you proved yourself worthy. But as you hear the truth of His grace repeatedly, your perspective shifts. You begin thinking differently about Him, and that's repentance.

And here's what I've discovered: when your mind changes about who God is, everything else in your life changes too. If you see Him as stingy, you'll live in fear of lack. But when His Word reveals Him as generous, provision becomes your expectation. If you see Him as harsh and demanding, you'll live under condemnation. But when His Word shows Him as merciful and accepting, you walk in freedom. The person who discovers God isn't angry grows generous because they've encountered a generous Father. The person who realizes God is merciful becomes merciful because they've experienced His mercy. This transformation doesn't come from trying harder to act like God. It flows naturally from changing your mind about who He is.

How the Word Works in You

When you consistently hear, believe, and speak Scripture, it begins transforming you in several ways:

It Renews Your Mind: Romans 12:2 says, "Be transformed by the renewing of your mind." Many believers have heard this verse countless times, but have never been told how this renewal actually happens. They know they're supposed to have a renewed mind, but they don't know what the process looks like or how to tell if it's working. This confusion creates anxiety and striving, as believers try to force their minds to think differently through sheer willpower.

Here's the liberating truth: the hear-believe-speak-receive pattern IS the process of renewing your mind. You're not trying to renovate your thinking through mental discipline or positive psychology. Mind renewal happens as you consistently expose yourself to God's Word, believe what it says about Him and about you, speak those truths, and receive the transformation the Word produces.

As you hear God's Word about who He really is, your mind is transformed. When you consistently hear about the Father's love, His grace, His abundant mercy, His eagerness to provide and heal, your thinking changes. You stop seeing Him as a disappointed taskmaster keeping score of your failures. You stop viewing Him as a harsh judge waiting to punish your mistakes. Instead, you begin seeing Him as the loving Father He truly is, one who delights in you, who eagerly provides for you, who runs toward you rather than away from you.

The pattern also renews your sense of identity. As you hear repeatedly that you are righteous in Christ, that the old man was crucified, that you are a new creation, that you are loved unconditionally, your thinking about yourself transforms. You stop identifying with your failures and start identifying with Christ's victory. You stop seeing yourself through the lens of past mistakes and start seeing yourself through the lens of God's grace.

This transformation doesn't happen overnight, and it doesn't require you to understand every theological detail. You simply engage in the pattern: hear God's Word about His character and your identity, believe it despite your feelings and circumstances, speak it over yourself and your situations, and receive the renewed thinking that the Word produces. The Word itself does the renewing work. You're not forcing your mind to think differently; you're allowing God's truth to reshape your thinking from the inside out.

You'll know mind renewal is happening when you notice yourself responding differently to situations than you used to. When someone criticizes you and instead of spiraling into shame, you remember your identity in Christ. When symptoms attack your body, and instead of accepting defeat, your mind goes to the healing promises in God's Word. These aren't responses you manufacture through effort; they're the natural result of a mind that's been renewed through consistent exposure to God's truth.

So if you've been wondering how to renew your mind, whether you're doing it right, or what the endpoint looks like, stop striving. You're already in the process. Every time you hear God's Word, every time you choose to believe it, every time you speak it, every time you position yourself to receive what it promises, your mind is being renewed. Not by your effort, but by the living, active Word of God doing its transforming work in you.

It Changes Your Heart: Psalm 119:11 declares, "Your word I have hidden in my heart, that I might not sin against You." When God's Word fills your heart through consistent hearing and believing, the Scripture stored in your heart becomes the source of right desires. You don't have to force yourself to want what God wants; the Word working in your heart naturally produces godly desires. You're not trying to manufacture holiness; the Word is creating a holy heart that naturally produces holy living.

This is completely different from behavior modification. Think about someone who struggles with bitterness and unforgiveness. They might try white-knuckling their way to forgiveness, forcing themselves to say the right words while their heart still burns with resentment. But when that same person consistently hears about the Father's unconditional forgiveness toward them, about how Christ bore their sins without holding grudges, about the freedom that comes from releasing others, something shifts inside. The Word doesn't just change what they think; it changes what they want. Their heart softens. Forgiveness stops being a painful duty and becomes a natural response. That's the Word changing the heart.

You'll know your heart is being changed when you notice your desires shifting. Maybe you find yourself genuinely wanting to pray instead of seeing it as an obligation. Or you discover generosity flowing naturally where stinginess once lived. Perhaps you notice compassion for others rising up where judgment used to dominate. These aren't changes you force through religious discipline. They are evidence that God's Word is doing its transforming work at the deepest level of who you are. The heart change produces the life change, and the Word produces the heart change.

It Builds Faith: Romans 10:17 reminds us that "faith comes by hearing, and hearing by the Word of God." Each time you hear God's truth, your faith capacity increases. This isn't about working up more faith through mental effort; it's about faith naturally growing as you expose yourself to the Word. Just as a plant grows when exposed to sunlight, your faith grows when exposed to Scripture. You're not striving to believe more. You're simply allowing the Word to do its work of building your faith.

But faith isn't passive; it's your primary weapon of defense. Ephesians 6:16 says, "Above all, taking the shield of faith with which you will be able to quench all the fiery darts of the wicked one." Notice it says "above all". Faith is the most critical piece of your spiritual armor. When the enemy launches accusations ("You're not really healed," "God's abandoned you," "You'll never overcome this"), faith built through God's Word becomes the shield that stops those attacks cold. The doubt-filled thought hits your shield of faith and falls powerless to the ground.

This is why consistent hearing matters so much. Every time you hear God's Word, you're not just gaining information; you're reinforcing your shield. When you've heard repeatedly that you are righteous in Christ, the enemy's condemnation can't penetrate. When you've heard again and again that God works all things for your good, anxiety's fiery darts lose their power. When you've saturated yourself in promises of God's provision, fear of lack bounces off harmlessly. The Word doesn't just tell you to have faith; it builds the very faith that protects you from every attack the enemy throws at you.

It Produces Fruit: Isaiah 55:11 promises, *"So shall My word be that goes forth from My mouth; it shall not return to Me void, but it shall accomplish what I please, and it shall prosper in the thing for which I sent it."* Notice this doesn't say you will accomplish what God pleases through your effort; it says the Word itself will accomplish it. The Word contains within itself the power to produce the fruit God intended. Your job is to receive it and allow it to work.

What does this fruit look like? Galatians 5:22-23 describes the fruit of the Spirit: love, joy, peace, patience, kindness, goodness, faithfulness, gentleness, and self-control. Paul says that when you "walk in the Spirit," these qualities naturally appear, not through human effort. And here's the beautiful connection: the Spirit works through the Word. Jesus said, "The words that I speak to you are spirit, and they are life" (John 6:63). When you consistently hear God's Word about the Father's unconditional love, the Spirit produces love in you. When you hear promises about the peace Christ purchased, the Spirit cultivates peace in your heart even in chaos. When you hear about God's faithfulness, the Spirit makes you faithful. The Word is the seed, the Spirit is the life-giving power that causes it to grow. You're not trying to manufacture spiritual fruit through discipline. You're receiving the Word, and the Spirit is using it to produce His fruit in you.

Some fruit appears quickly, and other fruit develops gradually. You might hear a promise about healing and see immediate results. Or you might hear promises about provision and watch God's faithfulness unfold over months as He opens doors you didn't even know existed. You might notice the fruit of patience appearing in situations that used to unsettle you or discover gentleness replacing harshness in your speech without you consciously trying to change. Don't be discouraged if transformation seems slow in certain areas. The Word is working. Trust the process. The same Word that spoke creation into existence is speaking transformation into your life, and it will not return void.

Patience in the Process

One crucial aspect of receiving is understanding God's timing. Some promises manifest quickly, others unfold over months or years. Your job isn't to figure out the timeline; it's to keep believing and speaking God's truth regardless of how long it takes.

Abraham waited at least 15 years between God's promise of a son and Isaac's birth. During that time, he was "strengthened in faith, giving glory to God, and being fully convinced that what He had promised He was also able to perform" (Romans 4:20-21). But Abraham wasn't the only one who received through faith and patience. Hebrews 11:11 tells us, "By faith Sarah herself also received strength to conceive seed, and she bore a child when she was past the age, because she judged Him faithful who had promised."

Notice that Sarah received natural strength, actual physical ability that her aged body no longer possessed, by faith. The Word of God working in her produced tangible results in her physical body. This is the power of receiving God's Word; it doesn't just change your perspective or attitude, it can produce real, measurable change in your circumstances and even in your physical body.

Yet we must also acknowledge an important reality: you may face situations where you faithfully apply this pattern, hear-believe-speak-receive, and the specific outcome you're praying for doesn't manifest in the way or timing you expected. Perhaps you're believing for healing, and the sickness doesn't leave. Maybe you're standing on promises of provision, and the financial breakthrough doesn't come when you need it. Perhaps you're trusting God to restore a relationship, that remains broken.

Does this mean the process failed? Does it mean God's Word doesn't work? Absolutely not. Here's what this pattern secures: even when the specific outcome differs from your expectation, you can remain confident that Romans 8:28 is true, "all things work together for good to those who love God, to those who are called according to His purpose." And you can experience the reality of Philippians 4:7, that "the peace of God, which surpasses all understanding, will guard your hearts and minds through Christ Jesus."

The Word working in you produces peace that transcends your circumstances. It builds confidence in God's goodness even when you don't understand His ways. It creates trust in His character when His methods confound you. You may not receive the exact answer you wanted, but you will receive the grace to walk through whatever comes with unshakeable faith in your Father's love and wisdom.

This is still receiving. Sometimes what we receive is different from what we asked for, but it's always what we need. The Word doing its work in you guarantees that you won't be destroyed by disappointment, won't be crushed by unanswered questions, and won't lose your faith when circumstances don't align with your prayers. You'll walk through the fire without being burned, through the flood without being overwhelmed, because God's Word has done its work of establishing you on the solid rock of His faithfulness.

Cooperating with Grace

While you can't make God's Word work through effort, you can cooperate with its working through faith. This cooperation isn't about adding human effort to make God's promises happen. It's about creating the environment where God's Word can freely accomplish what it was sent to do. Think of God's Word like fire — once ignited in your heart through hearing and believing, it spreads naturally. You don't create the flame through striving, and you can't make it burn brighter through willpower. Your cooperation is simply this: don't quench it. 1 Thessalonians 5:19 warns, 'Do not quench the Spirit.' When you consistently hear God's truth, choose to believe it despite contrary circumstances, speak it over your situations, and maintain an attitude of faith-filled expectation, you're providing oxygen to the flame. The Word itself does the burning - consuming lies, illuminating truth, and warming your heart with transformation.

You don't quench the Spirit through moral failure or imperfect performance. You quench it by refusing to engage with grace - by neglecting to hear God's Word, choosing not to believe what He says about you, speaking contrary to His truth, or failing to position yourself to receive what He's freely giving.

Remember what we learned in Chapter 4 about the power of your words: death and life are in the power of the tongue. When you consistently speak defeat over your circumstances, when you declare 'I'll never change' or 'This situation is hopeless,' when you agree with the enemy's lies about your identity rather than God's truth, you're throwing water on the fire. You're not sinning yourself out of God's grace, but you are quenching the Spirit's work in your heart. The flame of God's Word is still there, still ready to ignite transformation, but your contrary words create an environment where the fire struggles to spread.

This is why cooperating with grace is so crucial. Keep hearing. Keep believing. Keep speaking God's truth. Keep positioning yourself to receive. You're not making the fire burn through your effort; you're simply not quenching what God has already ignited in you.

This is the beauty of grace: the pressure is off. You're not responsible for making transformation happen, for manufacturing enough faith, or for figuring out how to bring God's promises to pass. The Word works because behind every promise stands the character and faithfulness of God Himself. He cannot lie, His Word will not return void, and what He has spoken will come to pass. You're not trusting in methods or formulas, you're trusting in the One who cannot fail and whose Word never returns void.

Your cooperation is simply this: keep your heart open to His Word, keep your mind focused on His truth, keep your mouth speaking His promises, and keep your spirit expecting His goodness. The Word will do the rest.

Bridging the Gap: Receiving Through Grace – The Word Does The Work

You don't produce transformation through self-effort. You receive it as God's Word works in your heart to renew your mind, build faith, and produce fruit. Scripture is like a flame that ignites wherever it touches: when you expose yourself to God's Word through hearing and believing, it naturally spreads through your thoughts, emotions, and actions, transforming everything it reaches. The Word does the work; your role is simply not to quench it.

CHAPTER 6:

WHEN THE PATTERN WORKS - AND WHEN IT FAILS

Joshua, Caleb, and the Ten Spies

Now that you understand the complete hear-believe-speak-receive pattern, let's see it in action—both when it works and when it fails. Numbers 13-14 gives us one of the most sobering case studies in all of Scripture.

What happens when someone *hears* the Word but doesn't *believe* it? What happens when people abort the pattern before it completes?

Twelve men went into Canaan to spy out the land God had already promised to give Israel. They all saw the same land, heard the same promise, and faced the same giants. But only two received what God offered.

Same Promise, Different Results

The story begins with God's clear directive to Moses: "Send men to spy out the land of Canaan, which I am giving to the children of Israel" (Numbers 13:2). Notice the tense: "I am giving." Not "I will give" or "I might give." Present tense. The transaction was already complete in God's eternal perspective - Israel just needed to walk in and possess it.

Moses sent twelve tribal leaders, one from each tribe, to reconnoiter the land. His instructions were strategic: "See what the land is like: whether the people who dwell in it are strong or weak, few or many; whether the land they dwell in is good or bad; whether the cities they inhabit are like camps or strongholds" (Numbers 13:18-19).

Notice what Moses *didn't* say. He didn't say, "See *if* we can take it." The assumption was that God had already handled the "if." Their job was intelligence gathering, not feasibility assessment. They were supposed to report on what was there, not whether it was possible.

For forty days, they walked through their inheritance. They saw fruitfulness so extreme that a single cluster of grapes required two men to carry it on a pole (v. 23). They observed fortified cities, diverse peoples, and abundant resources. Everything they saw was already theirs according to God's Word.

HEAR: The Same Promise for Everyone

Remember from chapter 2: faith comes by hearing. All twelve spies heard the same promise. God's Word to Israel was unambiguous: the land was theirs. The conquest wasn't contingent on their strength, strategy, or courage. God had spoken it into existence the moment He made the covenant with Abraham. Everything between that promise and its fulfillment was simply the *outworking* of what God had already decreed.

But here's the critical point: hearing the same Word doesn't guarantee believing the same Word. What you do with what you hear determines everything. The spies returned from identical experiences with radically different reports.

This principle still operates today. Two people can sit in the same church service, hear the same Scripture about healing, provision, or victory, and walk away with completely opposite conclusions. One leaves thinking, "That's mine - I receive it." The other thinks, "That sounds nice, but it's not for me." Same Word. Different belief. Completely different outcomes.

BELIEVE: Where the Pattern Splits

This is exactly what we explored in Chapter 3. Belief is choosing God's truth over what you see, feel, or experience. Watch how the pattern splits, or departs from God's intended outcome into failure.

When the spies returned to the congregation, ten of them issued what Scripture calls "a bad report" (Numbers 13:32). Their assessment was unanimous and damning:

> *"We are not able to go up against the people, for they are stronger than we... The land through which we have gone as spies is a land that devours its inhabitants, and all the people whom we saw in it are men of great stature. There we saw the giants (the descendants of Anak came from the giants); and we were like grasshoppers in our own sight, and so we were in their sight." (Numbers 13:31-33)*

Notice their focus: "We are not able... we were like grasshoppers in our own sight."

They looked at *themselves*. They measured *their* strength against the obstacles. They calculated from a human perspective and concluded that defeat was inevitable before the battle even began. The phrase "in our own sight" is devastating - they didn't evaluate reality based on God's promise; they evaluated reality based on their self-perception.

And once they saw themselves as grasshoppers, they assumed that's how the giants saw them, too. Their internal narrative became their external reality. This is exactly how unbelief works: it projects our fears onto our circumstances and treats those projections as facts.

But Joshua and Caleb heard the same promise and came to the opposite conclusion:

> *"Let us go up at once and take possession, for we are well able to overcome it." (Numbers 13:30)*

> *"The land we passed through to spy out is an exceedingly good land. If the LORD delights in us, then He will bring us into this land and give it to us... Only do not rebel against the LORD, nor fear the people of the land, for they*

are our bread; their protection has departed from them, and the LORD is with us. Do not fear them." (Numbers 14:7-9)

Notice their focus: "The LORD will bring us... The LORD is with us."

They looked at *God.* They measured the giants against God's promise. They calculated from a divine perspective and expected victory. When they said "they are our bread," they meant the giants represented nothing more threatening than a meal, consumable, useful, destined to strengthen them rather than destroy them.

The Root of Unbelief

The writer of Hebrews later explains what went wrong: "So we see that they could not enter in because of unbelief" (Hebrews 3:19). It wasn't a lack of military might. It wasn't the size of the giants or the fortification of the cities. It was *unbelief* - refusing to believe what God said about their identity and their inheritance.

Unbelief isn't simply the absence of faith. It's the active rejection of God's Word in favor of human reasoning. The ten spies didn't say, "We're not sure if we can do this." They said, "We are not able." That's not uncertainty - that's a definitive conclusion that contradicts God's definitive promise.

This is why unbelief is so serious. It's not a minor failing or a personality quirk. It's calling God a liar. When God says, "I am giving you this land," and you respond, "No, You're not - it's impossible," you've positioned yourself against Him.

SPEAK: Your Words Seal Your Destiny

Chapter 4 showed us the power of our words, and here we see it in stark relief. The ten spies didn't just believe wrong - they spoke wrong. And their words spread like poison through the entire camp:

> *"They gave the children of Israel a bad report of the land... and all the congregation lifted up their voices and cried, and the people wept that night." (Numbers 13:32; 14:1)*

Within hours, two million people shifted from anticipation to despair. Their unbelief became corporate. Their words created an atmosphere so thick with fear and defeat that even Moses and Aaron fell on their faces before the assembly (14:5). When Joshua and Caleb tried to correct the narrative, "all the congregation said to stone them with stones" (14:10).

But here's where the story becomes sobering. God Himself responds to their words:

> *"Say to them, 'As I live,' says the LORD, 'just as you have spoken in My hearing, so I will do to you.'" (Numbers 14:28)*

Read that again. "Just as you have spoken... so I will do to you."

They said, "We cannot take the land." God said, "Fine. You won't."

They said, "Our children will become victims." God said, "Actually, your children will inherit what you rejected, but you will die in the wilderness."

They said, "If only we had died in this wilderness!" (14:2). God said, "Granted. The carcasses of you who have complained against Me shall fall in this wilderness" (14:29).

Your words matter. They don't create reality out of nothing - only God's Word does that. But your words align you with either God's truth or the enemy's lies. The ten spies spoke themselves out of their inheritance. They traded the Promised Land for a mass grave, and it happened because of what they said.

Meanwhile, Joshua and Caleb kept speaking differently. Even when the congregation wanted to stone them, they declared: "The land is exceedingly good... the LORD is with us... do not fear" (14:7-9). Their words aligned with God's Word. And ultimately, their words determined their destiny.

RECEIVE: The Pattern Completes (or Aborts)

Chapter 5 taught us that receiving happens as God's Word works in you. But what if you abort the pattern before it completes?

The Ten Spies: They never received the Promised Land. They wandered in the wilderness for 38 more years until their generation died off - one year for every day they spent spying out the land they refused to possess (14:34). They spent four decades circling around the very blessing God had already given them, all because they heard but didn't believe, and spoke death instead of life.

Their journey became a cautionary tale for all future generations. Psalm 95:10-11 records God's verdict: "For forty years I was grieved with that generation... So I swore in My wrath, 'They shall not enter My rest.'" The rest was available. The land was theirs. But they forfeited it through unbelief.

Joshua and Caleb: They entered. They conquered. They received their inheritance.

Forty-five years after this incident, when Caleb was 85 years old, he stood before Joshua and made this remarkable declaration:

> *"As yet I am as strong this day as on the day that Moses sent me; just as my strength was then, so now is my strength for war, both for going out and for coming in. Now therefore, give me this mountain of which the LORD spoke in that day... It may be that the LORD will be with me, and I shall be able to drive them out as the LORD said." (Joshua 14:11-12)*

Notice: Caleb was still speaking the same word, still believing the same promise, still expecting the same result. The pattern never stopped for him. He kept hearing ("the LORD spoke"), kept believing ("the LORD will be with me"), kept speaking ("give me this mountain"), and kept receiving - all the way into fullness.

Forty-five years. Through wilderness wandering, watching his generation die off, enduring delay after delay. But he never stopped working the pattern. And when the time finally came, he claimed his mountain and drove out the giants just as God had promised.

The Lesson: The Pattern Always Works When You Work the Pattern

This story demolishes the excuse, "Well, I believed, but it didn't work."

Did you really believe? Or did you calculate impossibility like the ten spies?

Did you speak God's truth? Or did you agree with the circumstances and spread a "bad report"?

Did you persist in faith through delay? Or did you give up when you didn't see immediate results?

The pattern works. God's Word works. The question is whether you'll work the pattern all the way through.

The ten spies aborted the pattern at "believe." They heard but didn't believe. Therefore, they spoke wrongly and received death instead of life.

Joshua and Caleb completed the pattern. They heard, they believed, despite massive opposition, they spoke truth in the face of fear, and they received everything God promised - even if it took 45 years.

The pattern doesn't fail. People fail to work the pattern.

Application: Which Report Will You Believe?

Right now, God has promises for you. He's already given you everything that pertains to life and godliness through the knowledge of Him (2 Peter 1:3). You have an inheritance in Christ - healing, provision, peace, victory, abundant life. These aren't aspirational goals; they're current realities purchased by Jesus' finished work.

But between you and the manifestation of those promises, there are "giants" - circumstances that seem impossible, obstacles that appear insurmountable, voices (maybe even your own) that say, "You can't. It's too big. You're not enough."

You have a choice.

You can look at yourself and say, "I'm like a grasshopper. I'm not enough. This is too big for me." You can speak defeat, spread fear to everyone around you, and spend the rest of your life wandering around blessings God already provided, but you never possessed.

Or you can look at Jesus and say, "The LORD is with me. What He has promised, He is able to perform. These giants are bread - they're nothing compared to my God." You can speak faith, persist in truth despite what you see, and walk into your inheritance.

Same promise. Different perspective. Completely different outcome.

The ten spies saw giants and felt like grasshoppers. Joshua and Caleb saw the same giants and declared them to be consumed. The difference wasn't the size of the opposition - it was the size of their God in their perspective.

Which report will you believe?

What will you speak?

What will you receive?

The pattern works. Now work the pattern.

Bridging the Gap: The Pattern Works – And When It Fails

The pattern always works when you work the pattern, but it can be aborted at any step. Joshua and Caleb heard God's promise, believed despite the giants, spoke faith for 45 years, and received their inheritance, while the ten spies heard the same promise but looked at themselves instead of God, spoke defeat, and died in the wilderness. Same promise, different perspective, completely different outcome.

So we see that they could not enter in because of unbelief.

Hebrews — 3:19

CHAPTER 7:

WHAT JESUS ACCOMPLISHED - THE FOUNDATION OF EVERY PROMISE

To understand the full scope of what's available to you as a new creation, you need to grasp what Jesus accomplished when He was crucified. Isaiah 53, written 700 years before Christ's birth, prophetically describes the comprehensive work of the cross that makes every promise in God's Word possible for you.

This isn't just about salvation for heaven; it's about the abundant life Jesus promised. Every struggle you face, every need you have, every area where the old man tries to resurface was dealt with at Calvary.

But here's what's crucial: you cannot believe what you haven't heard, and you cannot receive what you're unaware of. This is why hearing about what Jesus accomplished is perhaps the most important thing you can fill your heart with. When you consistently hear the truth about the exchange that took place at the cross, when these realities become the meditation of your heart, faith rises naturally. You're not trying to work up belief in God's promises; you're simply hearing what Jesus already did, and faith comes alive in response to that hearing.

As we know, "faith comes by hearing, and hearing by the word of God." In this chapter, we're going to hear about the most foundational truth in all of Scripture: what Jesus accomplished for you. As you read these words, you're not just gaining information; you're positioning yourself to receive the faith-building power that comes from hearing about Christ's finished work. Let these truths sink deep into your heart. This is what you need to hear again and again until it becomes more real to you than any circumstance you're facing.

But before we dive into Isaiah 53 and walk through everything Jesus accomplished at the cross, we need to make one important stop first. Because if you approach the exchange principle with the wrong heart posture, you'll turn grace into a transaction. You'll read Isaiah 53 as a spiritual contract rather than a love letter. You'll focus on what you can get from Jesus instead of who Jesus is.

So let's start where transformation actually begins: by simply beholding Him.

Falling in Love Changes Everything

Second Corinthians 3:18 reveals a profound truth about transformation: "But we all, with unveiled face, beholding as in a mirror the glory of the Lord, are being transformed into the same image from glory to glory, just as by the Spirit of the Lord."

We are transformed by beholding. Not by trying harder. Not by following rules. Not by claiming promises. By beholding Jesus.

And here's what gets lost when we focus solely on what Jesus accomplished FOR us: simply beholding who Jesus IS transforms you.

Watch Him stoop down to embrace children while His disciples try to shoo them away. See Him sit by a well in the heat of the day, breaking every social rule to offer living water to a Samaritan woman with a broken past. Notice Him reach out and touch a leper—something no one else would do—and say, "I am willing." Observe Him stand between an adulteress and her accusers, drawing in the sand while religious men clutch their stones.

This is 2 Corinthians 3:18 in action: transformation through beholding. Not beholding a transaction but beholding a Person. Not analyzing what He did for you, but falling in love with who He is.

See Jesus rebuking the Pharisees for putting burdens on people. You realize He hates religion that crushes rather than liberates. Watch Him weep at Lazarus' tomb. You discover He doesn't stand distant from your pain. Observe Him washing His disciples' feet. You encounter a God who serves rather than demands service. Hear Him say "Father, forgive them" while nails pierce His hands. You meet a love that defies comprehension.

Something happens when you simply gaze at Jesus being Jesus. You're not trying to extract a healing or claim a promise. You're just watching Him. Listening to Him. Seeing how He treats the broken, the outcast, the religious, the desperate, the proud, and the humble. And as you behold Him, you fall in love. And falling in love changes you in ways that trying to change yourself never could.

The woman caught in adultery wasn't transformed because Jesus healed her body or gave her money. She was transformed because she beheld grace personified, looking at her with eyes that held no condemnation. The Samaritan woman didn't change because of what she got from Jesus. She changed because of who she encountered; Someone who saw all her shame and offered living water still.

This is why reading the Gospels matters so profoundly. Not just to learn what Jesus did, but to watch Him do it. Not just to catalogue His miracles, but to witness His heart. Behold Him enough, and you can't help but be transformed into His likeness. Not because you're trying to be like Him, but because love does what rules never could.

Before you rush to Isaiah 53 to claim your healing or provision, spend time in the Gospels just watching Jesus love people. Let yourself fall in love with Him. Because when you truly love Him, receiving what He purchased becomes the natural overflow of a relationship, not the manipulative transaction of religion

The Comprehensive Work of the Cross

Now, with hearts full of love for who Jesus is, let's see the full scope of what He accomplished for us at the cross. Let's walk through Isaiah 53:3-12 and see a fuller picture of what Jesus bore so you could be free. As you read each of these statements, don't rush past them. Hear them. Let them sink into your heart. This is the Word of God about what your Savior accomplished for you:

"He was despised and rejected by men, a Man of sorrows and acquainted with grief." (v. 3)

Hear this: Jesus experienced rejection so you could be accepted. He endured the pain of being despised so you could know you're valued by God. When you struggle with feelings of rejection or unworthiness, you need to hear this truth repeatedly: He took that so you wouldn't have to carry it. Every time you feel rejected, return to hearing this. Let it fill your heart until rejection loses its power over you because you know Jesus bore it in your place.

"Surely He has borne our grief and carried our sorrows." (v. 4)

Hear this carefully: The Hebrew words for "grief" and "sorrows" encompass physical sickness, emotional pain, and mental anguish. Jesus didn't just die for your sins; He carried your depression, your anxiety, your chronic pain, your grief over loss. This isn't theoretical theology; it's the foundation for your healing. When symptoms attack your body, when anxiety grips your mind, when sorrow threatens to overwhelm you, you need to hear this truth: Jesus already bore it. He already carried it. It's not yours to carry anymore.

"But He was wounded for our transgressions, He was bruised for our iniquities; the chastisement for our peace was upon Him, and by His stripes we are healed." (v. 5)

Hear the substitutionary nature of what happened: He was wounded so you could be whole. He was bruised, so you could be healthy. He took your punishment so you could have peace. By His stripes, not by your striving, not by your worthiness, not by your perfect faith, but by His stripes, you ARE healed. Present tense. Already accomplished. This is what you need to hear until it becomes more real to you than any symptom, any diagnosis, and any circumstance.

The Exchange Principle

Throughout Scripture, we see a divine exchange taking place. Jesus took what was ours so we could receive what is His. Hear these exchanges. Speak them aloud. Let them become the meditation of your heart:

He had no beauty → so you could be beautiful.

He was despised → so you could be loved and valued.

He was rejected → so you could be accepted.

He bore sorrow → so you could have joy.

He carried grief → so you could have comfort.

He was wounded → so you could be healed.

He was chastised → so you could have peace.

He carried iniquity → so you could be righteous.

He was judged → so you could be justified.

He was killed → so you could have an abundant life.

He became poor → so you could be enriched.

This is what you need to hear. Not once, not occasionally, but repeatedly until these truths become the foundation of how you see yourself and your circumstances. Every promise in God's Word flows from one of these exchanges. Every need you have was addressed at the cross through this divine transaction.

When sickness attacks, you need to hear: "He was wounded so I could be healed. By His stripes I am healed." Hear it until your faith rises above your symptoms, not through gritting your teeth and trying to believe harder, but simply from the natural result of hearing God's truth about what Jesus accomplished.

When anxiety grips you, you need to hear: "He was chastised so I could have peace." The peace isn't something you manufacture through deep breathing and positive thinking; it's something you receive as you hear about the exchange that already took place.

This is why the hear-believe-speak-receive pattern is so powerful. When you consistently hear about what Jesus accomplished, belief naturally follows. You're not trying to talk yourself into believing something that seems impossible; you're simply responding with faith to what you've heard about what Christ already did. And as you believe it and speak it, you position yourself to receive what the exchange provides.

Why Beholding the Exchange Changes Everything

Now that you've spent time simply watching Jesus love people—letting yourself fall in love with who He is—you're ready to see the full scope of what He accomplished for you. And here's where 2 Corinthians 3:18 reveals another dimension: beholding "as in a mirror."

When you look in a mirror, you see yourself reflected. But when you behold Jesus in Isaiah 53, something remarkable happens: you see the exchange from both sides simultaneously.

You see what He took from you and what you received from Him. You see your sickness in Him and His healing in you. You see your poverty on Him and His wealth transferred to you. The mirror shows you both realities at once: His substitution and your inheritance.

This is why many believers struggle to receive what the cross purchased. They behold their sin on Jesus (substitution) but fail to behold His righteousness on them (inheritance). They see Him carrying their sickness, but don't see themselves carrying His health. They acknowledge the transfer of their debt but never consider the deposit of His riches into their account.

Beholding the exchange means looking at both sides of the transaction. Read "He was wounded for our transgressions". Don't stop at seeing Him wounded. Behold yourself made whole. Read "He bore our grief." Don't stop at seeing Him carrying. Behold yourself freed from carrying. Read "He became poor". Don't stop there. Behold yourself enriched.

This is the mirror of 2 Corinthians 3:18. It reflects both the taking and the giving, both the bearing and the releasing, both the poverty and the wealth. Until you behold both sides of the exchange, you'll remain stuck trying to earn what's already been transferred to your account.

Why This Matters for Your Daily Life

Understanding what Jesus accomplished changes everything about how you approach your struggles and needs, but understanding alone isn't enough. You need to hear it. Repeatedly. Consistently. Until it becomes the dominant voice in your heart.

Anxiety tries to overwhelm you. Return to hearing that Jesus bore your anxiety so you could have His peace. Sickness attacks your body. Hear again and again that by His stripes you were healed 2,000 years ago. Fear rears its ugly head. Remember, He has given you a spirit of power, of love, and of a sound mind (2 Timothy 1:7).

God's Word reveals spiritual truth about healing, but we also live in bodies that break down and minds that struggle in a fallen world. God's grace includes the doctors, medications, and treatments He's provided. Seeking medical care is wisdom, not a lack of faith. This pattern works alongside medical treatment, not as a replacement for it.

This is why the Old Covenant approach of trying harder doesn't work. You can't overcome through your willpower what Jesus already overcame through His sacrifice. The solution isn't more effort; it's hearing more about what He already provided, believing what you hear, speaking it over your circumstances, and receiving by faith what the exchange made available.

Consider how this works practically. You wake up feeling sick. Your natural instinct focuses on the symptoms, analyzing how bad you feel and worrying about what might be wrong. But what if instead, you immediately began hearing Isaiah 53:4-5? Speak it aloud: "Surely He has borne my grief and carried my sorrows. He was wounded for my transgressions, He was bruised for my iniquities; the chastisement for my peace was upon Him, and by His stripes I am healed."

You're not denying the symptoms exist. You're choosing to hear what Jesus accomplished rather than focusing exclusively on what you're experiencing. As you hear these words, faith begins to rise. Not manufactured faith that you're striving to work up, but natural faith that comes from hearing God's Word about what Christ already did.

Bills piling up? Financial pressure mounting? Instead of spiraling into anxiety and rehearsing all the reasons why you'll never get ahead, hear 2 Corinthians 8:9: "For you know the grace of our Lord Jesus Christ, that though He was rich, yet for your sakes He became poor, that you through His poverty might become rich." Hear it. Speak it. Let it fill your heart. Not as a magic formula, but as the truth about what Jesus accomplished that builds faith for provision.

The exchange principle isn't just a doctrine to understand intellectually; it's the truth to hear repeatedly until it transforms how you see every circumstance. This is what Paul meant when he asked the Galatians, "Did you receive the Spirit by the works of the law, or by the hearing of faith?" (Galatians 3:2). Everything in the Christian life, every promise, every provision, every transformation, comes through hearing with faith, not through working with effort.

The Word Contains the Power

Every promise in Scripture is backed by the finished work of the cross. When you hear, believe, and speak God's Word about healing, provision, peace, or any other need, you're not trying to convince God to do something; you're receiving what Jesus already accomplished.

But here's the key: the Word itself contains the power. When you hear "By His stripes you are healed," you're not just hearing information about a past event. You're hearing a living Word that carries within it the healing power purchased at Calvary. When you hear "He became poor so you could be enriched," you're not just learning theology; you're accessing the provision that flows from that exchange.

This is why the foundational truth of Romans 10:17 is so crucial (and why I've referred to it repeatedly so far in the book): "Faith comes by hearing, and hearing by the word of God." You can't believe for healing if you haven't heard that Jesus bore your sicknesses. You can't have faith for provision if you haven't heard about the poverty-to-riches exchange. You can't receive peace if you haven't heard that He was chastised, so you could have it.

The hearing comes first. Always. Not because God is stingy and requires you to jump through hoops, but because this is how faith works. Faith is a response to hearing the truth about what God has already provided. You're not generating faith through mental effort; you're receiving faith as the natural result of hearing about Christ's finished work.

This is why filling your heart with the exchange principle is so vital. When your heart is full of hearing about what Jesus bore and what you received in return, believing becomes natural. Speaking flows easily. Receiving happens as a matter of course. But when your heart is empty of this truth, when you haven't consistently heard about the exchange, believing becomes a struggle, speaking feels forced, and receiving seems impossible.

Think of it like this: if I asked you to have faith for something you've never heard about, something that hasn't been promised, something that wasn't purchased at the cross, you'd have no foundation for faith. But when you've heard repeatedly that Jesus bore your sicknesses, carried your sorrows, took your poverty, and exchanged His peace for your punishment, you have solid ground to stand on. Your faith isn't based on wishful thinking or positive confession; it's based on what you've heard about what Jesus actually accomplished.

This is the pinnacle of understanding the hear-believe-speak-receive pattern. What you hear about the cross becomes the content of what you believe, the substance of what you speak, and the foundation of what you receive. The more you hear about what Jesus accomplished, the stronger your faith becomes, the more naturally the declarations flow, and the more confidently you receive what the exchange provided.

The Old Man Is Dead

Remember, every problem you face is connected to the old man who was crucified with Christ. You're not trying to fix that person; you're declaring that he's dead and living from your new creation identity.

Jesus really did "pin it all to the cross" so you could walk in freedom. The comprehensive nature of the gospel shows that an abundant life includes physical health, emotional wholeness, financial provision, relational blessing, and spiritual authority. But accessing this abundant life requires that you hear about it. Repeatedly. Consistently.

The old man carried sickness; Jesus bore it in your place. Hear that. The old man lived in poverty; Jesus became poor so you could be enriched. Hear that. The old man was rejected; Jesus was rejected so you could be accepted. Hear that. The old man was bound by sin; Jesus carried your iniquities, so you could walk in righteousness. Hear that.

Each time you hear about what Jesus accomplished, you're building faith in your new identity. You're not trying to become a new creation through effort. You're hearing about the new creation you already are through Christ's finished work. The more you hear it, the more naturally you'll live from it.

This is why we keep emphasizing the importance of hearing. You can't walk in freedom from something if you're constantly focused on yourself. But when you hear repeatedly about what Jesus did with that thing at the cross, freedom becomes your experience. The old man, with all his struggles, was crucified with Christ. That's not something you need to make happen through discipline and determination; it's something that already happened that you need to hear about until you believe it, speak it, and receive it as your reality.

Bridging the Gap - What Jesus Accomplished

Transformation begins by beholding Jesus. Watch Him love people in the Gospels until your heart falls in love with who He is. Once you've encountered His character, you're ready to see the full scope of what He accomplished at the cross: Jesus took your sickness, poverty, rejection, and death so you could receive His healing, abundance, acceptance, and life. Every promise in Scripture is backed by His finished work, and you access it not by earning but by beholding Him, and what He already accomplished.

"But we all, with unveiled face, beholding as in a mirror the glory of the Lord, are being transformed into the same image from glory to glory, just as by the Spirit of the Lord."

2 Corinthians 3:18

CHAPTER 8:

WALKING IN YOUR NEW IDENTITY - GRACE IN ACTION

The beautiful thing about your new creation identity is that you don't have to manufacture it, maintain it, or perform to keep it. You already are who God says you are. The "walking out" isn't about discipline or trying harder, it's about simply agreeing with what's already true and letting that reality influence your daily life.

This isn't another self-improvement program or list of spiritual disciplines you need to master. Remember, the New Covenant is believing what God says. Everything we discuss in this chapter flows from grace, not effort.

It's Already Done

Before we talk about any practical applications, let's establish this foundational truth: your transformation isn't dependent on your performance. You are a new creation because Jesus made you one, not because you follow certain steps. You are righteous because He made you righteous, not because you do everything right.

This removes all pressure and performance anxiety. You're not trying to achieve your new identity; you're simply discovering how to live from it. When you mess up, you don't lose your identity. When you forget to "do" something, you're still who God says you are.

This truth is liberating beyond measure. Your identity in Christ isn't based on your latest spiritual performance review. It's not contingent on whether you had a good, quiet time this morning or whether you lost your temper this afternoon. When you sin, when you fail, when you fall back into old patterns, you remain a new creation in Christ. You remain righteous. You remain beloved. You remain accepted.

The enemy wants you to believe that your identity fluctuates based on your behavior, that you're only truly God's child when you're acting like it, that righteousness is something you achieve rather than something you've been given. But this is a lie designed to keep you bound to performance-based living. Your identity was established at the cross and sealed when you believed. Nothing you do or don't do changes that fundamental reality. You don't earn your identity through good days and lose it through bad days. It's already done, permanently established, forever settled.

How Grace Changes Everything

Under the Old Covenant mindset, daily spiritual life becomes a checklist: "Did I read my Bible? Did I pray enough?" This approach leads to either pride or condemnation.

Under the New Covenant, daily spiritual life becomes a relationship: "What is God saying to me? How is His Word working in my heart?" This approach leads to freedom and growth because it's based on what He's doing, not what you're doing.

This distinction is crucial. When your focus is on what you're doing, you're constantly evaluating your performance, measuring your progress, and assessing whether you did enough today to maintain your standing with God. Did you pray long enough? Was your Bible reading deep enough? Did you serve enough? Did you give enough? This creates an exhausting cycle of self-assessment that never brings peace because there's always more you could have done.

But when your focus shifts to what He's doing, everything changes. You're no longer the source of your spiritual growth; He is. You're not producing transformation through your discipline; His Word is working transformation in you. You're not generating love, joy, and peace through effort; the Holy Spirit is producing fruit in you as you stay connected to Christ. The pressure is off because you're cooperating with His work rather than trying to accomplish it through your own strength. This creates freedom because you're no longer burdened with producing your own growth; you're simply positioning yourself to receive what He's already doing.

Natural Responses to God's Grace

When you truly understand that you're already loved, accepted, and blessed, certain responses happen naturally, not because you force them, but because they flow from a grateful heart:

You Want to Hear His Voice: When you know someone loves you completely, you want to hear from them. Reading Scripture becomes less like a duty and more like receiving love letters.

You Find Yourself Speaking Differently: When your heart is full of God's love and promises, different words come out of your mouth naturally.

You Expect Good Things: When you know your Father owns everything and loves you deeply, expecting His goodness becomes natural.

Consider 1 John 4:19: "We love Him because He first loved us." This verse reveals a profound truth about how grace works. You cannot manufacture love for God through effort and willpower. You can't fulfill the greatest commandment, "Love the Lord your God with all your heart, with all your soul, and with all your mind" (Matthew 22:37), through sheer determination and religious duty.

The love you're commanded to have for God isn't something you produce; it's something you return. He loved you first. He initiated. He poured His love into your heart. As you truly *receive* His love, letting it sink deep into your being through hearing about it repeatedly and meditating upon it, love for Him naturally flows back. You're not trying to love God; you're responding to being loved by God.

The same principle applies to loving others. You can't manufacture genuine love for difficult people through gritting your teeth and trying harder to be nice. But a heart full of the love God has poured into you, a heart that's received His unconditional acceptance and abundant grace, naturally overflows with love for others. You're not generating love through effort; you're sharing the love you've received.

This is why receiving His love is so crucial. You must first receive before you can return or extend. The command to love isn't a call to produce something through your own strength; it's an invitation to receive God's love so fully that it naturally overflows to Him and to others. Trying to love without first receiving His love means operating in the flesh, striving to fulfill a command through human effort. But positioning yourself to receive His love through hearing about it, believing it, and speaking it over yourself makes love the natural response of a grace-filled heart.

Working Out What God Works In

There's a verse in Philippians that often confuses believers, particularly when we've been emphasizing that salvation and transformation come through grace rather than works. Philippians 2:12-13 says: "Therefore, my beloved, as you have always obeyed, not as in my presence only, but now much more in my absence, work out your own salvation with fear and trembling; for it is God who works in you both to will and to do for His good pleasure."

At first glance, this sounds like Paul is adding works to salvation, suggesting that believers need to earn or maintain their salvation through effort. But look carefully at what he's actually saying. He's not telling you to work for your salvation, he's telling you to work out what God has worked in you.

The distinction is crucial. Working for salvation is Old Covenant thinking, trying to earn God's acceptance through your performance. Working out your salvation is New Covenant living, allowing what God has placed inside you to naturally express itself through your life.

Notice the progression in verse 13: "It is God who works in you both to will and to do for His good pleasure." God isn't just giving you a list of activities to perform and then leaving you to figure out how to do them. He's working in you, first giving you the desire (to will) and then the ability (to do). Even the want-to comes from Him. Even the power to accomplish it flows from His work in you, not from your self-generated discipline.

This is exactly what we've been describing throughout this book. As you engage in the hear-believe-speak-receive pattern, God's Word is transforming you. You're not manufacturing holiness through effort. You're not generating good works through willpower. Instead, God is producing both the desire and the ability to live righteously as natural by-products of His Word working in your heart.

Let's be clear: we're not saying that believing in God's Word leads to spiritual passivity or that grace eliminates good works from the Christian life. Quite the opposite. The fruit of believing God's Word is divine activities and good works that the Lord gives you both the desire and ability to perform. These aren't works you do to earn salvation or maintain your standing with God. They're the natural expression of a heart that has been transformed by hearing, believing, speaking, and receiving God's truth.

Think about how this plays out practically. A heart full of God's love, through consistently hearing about His grace, naturally wants to love others. You're not forcing yourself to be loving because it's a Christian duty. The desire to love wells up from within because God is working in you to will it. And as opportunities to demonstrate that love appear, you find you have the ability to follow through because God is also working in you to do it.

Repeated hearing about God's generosity and His provision for you makes generosity toward others flow naturally. You're not trying to work up enough faith to give sacrificially. The desire to give is produced by God working in you. And as you act on that desire, you discover that God supplies not just the willingness but also the resources and the joy in giving.

As God's Word renews your mind about your identity in Christ, righteous living becomes increasingly natural. You're not straining to avoid sin through sheer willpower. Instead, you find that you want different things than you used to want, and you have the power to make different choices than you used to make. God is working in you both to will and to do.

This is working out your salvation. Not earning it. Not maintaining it through performance. Simply allowing what God has worked inside you through His Word and Spirit to express itself outwardly through your life.

The good works aren't absent, they're abundant. But they flow from grace working in you, not from you working to impress God. In fact, this pattern produces more good works and obedience, not less; but works flowing from love rather than fear, from desire rather than duty. The son who truly grasps his Father's love works harder than the servant trying to earn approval, but he works with joy instead of anxiety, with freedom instead of bondage. This isn't permission for passivity; it's power for genuine transformation.

So you see good fruit in your life. You notice yourself serving others and responding with patience rather than anger. Generosity comes naturally. Worship flows freely. Don't think "Look at what I've accomplished." Instead, recognize "This is God working in me both to will and to do for His good pleasure." Give Him the glory for producing in you what you could never generate through self-effort.

And what about when you don't see as much fruit as you'd like? Old patterns still surface. You struggle to do what you know is right. Don't fall into condemnation and try harder through human effort. Instead, return to the pattern. Hear more of God's Word about His grace and your identity. Believe what He says, despite how you feel. Speak His truth over yourself. Position yourself to receive what He's working in you. Trust that as you do, God will produce both the desire and the ability to live in the good works He prepared beforehand for you to walk in (Ephesians 2:10).

This is the beauty of New Covenant living. You're not passively sitting back waiting for God to make you into a robot who automatically does everything perfectly. But neither are you striving in your own strength to produce righteousness through sheer determination. Instead, you're actively cooperating with what God is doing in you, working out what He's working in, allowing the pattern of hearing, believing, speaking, and receiving to produce its natural fruit of divine activities and Spirit-empowered good works.

Grace Is Not a License to Sin

As we emphasize the permanence of your righteous identity and the reality that you don't lose your standing with God when you fail, some believers become concerned. They worry that this teaching about grace gives people permission to sin freely without consequences. This concern is understandable, and Paul himself addressed it directly in Romans 6.

Let's be clear: God's grace is absolutely not a license to sin. But here's what's remarkable: when someone truly receives a revelation of grace, when they genuinely understand the depth of God's love and the completeness of their acceptance in Christ, sin becomes less and less of an issue in their life. Not because they're trying harder to avoid it, but because grace itself transforms the heart in ways that law never could.

Romans 6:14-15 addresses this directly: "For sin shall not have dominion over you, for you are not under law but under grace. What then? Shall we sin because we are not under law but under grace? Certainly not!" Notice the promise: when you are under grace, sin shall not have dominion over you. Grace doesn't give sin more power in your life; it severs sin's power over you.

This is the opposite of what many fear. The concern is that emphasizing grace will lead to more sin, but Scripture promises that grace leads to less sin. When you're under law; constantly focused on rules and regulations, sin actually gains strength. 1 Corinthians 15:56 reveals this truth: "The strength of sin is the law." Rules without the power to keep them only highlight your inability and increase your desire to break them. But grace provides both the acceptance you crave and the power to live differently.

Paul continues in Romans 6:16-18: "Do you not know that to whom you present yourselves slaves to obey, you are that one's slaves whom you obey, whether of sin leading to death, or of obedience leading to righteousness? But God be thanked that though you were slaves of sin, yet you obeyed from the heart that form of doctrine to which you were delivered. And having been set free from sin, you became slaves of righteousness."

Here's the reality: using grace as a license to sin is self-deception. Deliberately choosing to sin while thinking grace covers it means you're not walking in grace at all—you're yielding yourself to sin. Yield yourself to sin, and you become its servant. Sin leads to death: spiritual death, relational death, the death of joy, peace, and freedom. You can't play with sin and expect grace to shield you from its consequences.

But here's the glorious alternative: yield yourself to God's grace. Position yourself to hear His Word about your righteousness. Believe what He says about your new identity. Speak His truth over your life. Do these things, and you become a servant of righteousness. And righteousness leads to life—abundant life, the life Jesus promised in John 10:10.

The question isn't whether grace allows you to sin. The question is: are you yielding yourself to sin or to grace? True understanding of grace—genuinely grasping that you're already righteous, already accepted, already loved completely—diminishes sin's appeal. Why serve sin after tasting the freedom of serving righteousness? Why pursue temporary pleasure that leads to death when you have access to an abundant life?

This is why we've emphasized being Christ-conscious rather than sin-conscious throughout this book. Constant focus on your sins—cataloging failures, rehearsing mistakes—yields mental and emotional space to sin. But Christ-consciousness, awareness of His love, His righteousness in you, His complete acceptance, yields you to grace. And as Romans 6:14 promises, sin shall not have dominion over you.

Some people will still misuse grace. Paul knew this would happen, which is why he addressed it so directly. But the misuse of grace doesn't negate its power for those who genuinely receive it. True revelation of grace produces true transformation. Not overnight, not without any struggle, but progressively and surely as you continue to hear, believe, speak, and receive God's truth about who you are in Christ.

If you find yourself deliberately sinning and excusing it with "I'm under grace," stop and ask yourself honestly: Have I truly received a revelation of grace, or am I using theological language to justify behavior I know is wrong?

True grace transforms. If your understanding of grace isn't producing righteousness in your life, you haven't yet grasped what grace really is. Return to hearing God's Word about His love, His righteousness given to you, His power at work in you. Let true grace do its transforming work.

When Old Patterns Resurface

There will be times when you react from the old nature, speak words you regret, or fall back into negative thinking. This is normal and doesn't mean you're failing.

When old patterns show up:

Don't condemn yourself. Remember, "There is therefore now no condemnation to those who are in Christ Jesus." No condemnation means no condemnation.

Return to truth: Simply begin hearing God's Word about your situation again.

Receive grace: Ask for help and trust that God's grace is sufficient.

Keep moving forward: Don't camp out on mistakes, focus on who you are in Christ.

Here's a crucial principle: sin consciousness doesn't create righteous living. Being constantly aware of your sins, rehearsing your failures, and focusing on your shortcomings doesn't produce holiness, it produces condemnation and discouragement. Hebrews 10:2 reveals that Christ's sacrifice was designed to remove the consciousness of sin: "For then would they not have ceased to be offered? For the worshipers, once purified, would have had no more consciousness of sins." The Old Covenant sacrifices had to be repeated because they couldn't remove sin consciousness, but Christ's once-for-all sacrifice accomplished what the law never could. When you're constantly focused on your sin, you're living under Old Covenant consciousness. But when you're Christ-conscious, aware of who He is and what He's done, aware of your identity in Him and His righteousness bestowed upon you, you naturally produce the fruit of righteous living. Being Christ-conscious, not sin-conscious, is what transforms your behavior from the inside out.

The Long View

Walking in your new identity is a journey, not a destination. There will always be new areas to grow in, fresh challenges that test your faith, and deeper levels of God's truth to discover. But you don't have to figure it all out at once.

Focus on the process, not perfection. Celebrate small victories, times when you respond differently than you used to, when peace replaces anxiety, or when hope rises instead of discouragement. This is evidence that your new nature is becoming more dominant.

Trust that the same God who made you new is faithful to complete the work He started. Philippians 1:6 promises, "Being confident of this very thing, that He who has begun a good work in you will complete it until the day of Jesus Christ." Your job isn't to make transformation happen; it's to cooperate with what He's already doing through His Word and Spirit.

Walking in your new identity isn't about adding more disciplines to your life; it's about living from what's already true. You're not trying to become righteous through effort; you're living as the righteous person Christ made you. As you position yourself to hear God's Word, believe it, speak it, and receive it, transformation happens naturally through His grace working in you, not through your striving.

Bridging the Gap: Walking in Your New Identity - Grace in Action

You are already a new creation in Christ. Walking in your new identity isn't about achieving righteousness through discipline but living from the righteousness you've already been given. God doesn't want your performance; He wants you to receive revelation of who He is and who you are in Him, so that transformation flows naturally as His Word works in you both to will and to do. When you shift from performance evaluation to recognizing God's work in you, good works flow abundantly; not from striving, but from the overflow of grace.

Therefore, if anyone is in Christ, he is a new creation; old things have passed away; behold, all things have become new.

2 Corinthians 5:17

CHAPTER 9:

LIVING THE ABUNDANT LIFE - YOUR ONGOING JOURNEY

Jesus declared in John 10:10, "I have come that they may have life, and that they may have it more abundantly." This abundant life isn't just a promise for heaven; it's your inheritance right now as a new creation in Christ. Everything we've discussed in this book points toward this reality: God wants you to experience fullness of life in every area.

The abundant life isn't about having perfect circumstances; it's about having God's peace in any circumstances, His provision for every need, His healing for every hurt, and His strength for every challenge. It's about walking in your new-creation identity so consistently that abundance becomes your normal experience rather than an occasional blessing.

What Abundant Life Looks Like

Abundant life is characterized by several key elements that become increasingly evidcnt as you mature in the hear-believe-speak-receive lifestyle:

Spiritual Abundance: Deep intimacy with God, clear understanding of His Word, confidence in prayer, and natural overflow of His love to others.

Emotional Abundance: Peace that surpasses understanding, joy that doesn't depend on circumstances, hope that remains strong during trials, and love that extends even to enemies.

Physical Abundance: Divine health as your normal state, energy for God's purposes, healing when sickness tries to attack, and longevity to fulfill your calling.

Relational Abundance: Healthy marriages, blessed children, meaningful friendships, positive workplace relationships, and the ability to forgive and restore broken connections.

Financial Abundance: Having enough for your needs, resources to give generously, wisdom to manage money biblically, and freedom from financial anxiety.

Mental Abundance: Renewed thinking patterns, creative problem-solving, clear decision-making, and the mind of Christ in complex situations.

This isn't about perfection or the absence of challenges; it's about having God's resources available for whatever you face.

The Progression of Abundance

Abundant life typically develops in stages as you grow in faith and consistency with God's Word:

Stage 1: Crisis Response. Initially, you might only turn to God's Word during major problems. You hear, believe, speak, and receive primarily when circumstances force you to seek God desperately.

Stage 2: Proactive Application. As you see God's faithfulness, you begin applying His Word before crises hit. You start your day with Scripture, speak God's truth over upcoming challenges, and build faith for future needs.

Stage 3: Lifestyle Integration. Eventually, the hear-believe-speak-receive pattern becomes as natural as breathing. You automatically think from God's perspective, speak His truth, and expect His goodness in every situation.

Stage 4: Overflow Blessing. At this level, God's abundance in your life naturally blesses everyone around you. You become a conduit of His grace, and people are drawn to the life they see in you.

The Outflow of Abundance

As you experience God's abundance through the hear-believe-speak-receive pattern, it naturally overflows into every area of your life. This isn't something you force or manufacture; it's the organic result of a heart filled with God's truth and grace.

In your family, life-giving words may flow naturally over your spouse and children. An atmosphere of faith develops in your home as they hear you respond to challenges from God's perspective rather than human reasoning. Your peace becomes their peace, your hope becomes their hope.

In your workplace, you may become known for maintaining calm during stressful times. Your integrity in difficult decisions stands out. When others complain or worry, your positive outlook rooted in God's promises becomes a testimony without you having to preach.

In your community, opportunities to encourage others with God's truth seem to present themselves naturally. When people share their struggles, prayer flows easily. God's love expresses itself through acts of service and generosity that surprise even you.

Through your testimony, stories of how God's Word has worked in your life become a natural part of the conversation. You find yourself pointing people to Scripture rather than to yourself, showing them that the abundant life is available to anyone who will hear, believe, speak, and receive God's truth.

Heavenly Minded Through the Pattern

When Scripture commands you to "set your mind on things above, where Christ is, sitting at the right hand of God" (Colossians 3:1-2), this isn't another spiritual discipline to master or a mental exercise to perfect. This is simply what happens when you engage in the hear-believe-speak-receive pattern consistently.

Think about what you've been doing as you've walked through this book. You've been hearing God's Word about what Jesus accomplished at the cross. You've been believing promises about your new identity rather than the circumstances you see. You've been speaking God's truth over your situations instead of agreeing with natural limitations. You've been positioning yourself to receive what Christ has already provided. In doing all of this, you have been setting your mind on things above; you've been living from a heavenly perspective rather than an earthly one.

Romans 8:5-6 draws a stark contrast: "For those who live according to the flesh set their minds on the things of the flesh, but those who live according to the Spirit, the things of the Spirit. For to be carnally minded is death, but to be spiritually minded is life and peace." Being carnally minded means focusing exclusively on what you can see, feel, and measure in the natural realm. Your circumstances govern your thoughts. Your limitations define your expectations. What you lack controls your perspective.

But being spiritually minded means something entirely different. It means your thoughts are anchored in spiritual realities that transcend natural circumstances. You're aware of what Ephesians 1:3 declares: you have been "blessed with every spiritual blessing in the heavenly places in Christ." These blessings aren't waiting for you in some distant future; they exist right now in the heavenly realm. And through the hear-believe-speak-receive pattern, you're accessing what's already yours.

Consider what Ephesians 2:6 reveals about your current position: God "raised us up together, and made us sit together in the heavenly places in Christ Jesus." This isn't describing something that will happen when you die and go to heaven. This is your present reality. Right now, you are seated with

Christ in heavenly places. You're not climbing up to reach Him through spiritual disciplines and religious performance. You're already there, positioned with Him, sharing His victory, accessing His resources.

But what does this actually mean in the middle of an ordinary Tuesday? How do you live from your seated position when circumstances feel overwhelming?

Here's what the shift looks like: You hear a difficult diagnosis. Your initial reaction might be fear—that's human. But then you remember where you're seated. You're not under the circumstance; you're seated above it with Christ. As you hear God's Word about healing, as you believe those promises despite the medical report, as you speak from your position in Christ rather than from your anxiety, something changes. Not necessarily the circumstance (though it might), but your perspective. You're no longer at the mercy of the diagnosis. You're accessing the reality of your healing that exists in the heavenly realm, living from heaven's perspective rather than being trapped in earth's limitations.

The shift isn't about never feeling fear or denying reality. It's about where you ultimately anchor your thinking. Are you letting your circumstances have the final word, defining your reality and dictating your response? Or are you letting your position in Christ define your reality and shape your perspective? The person seated in heavenly places doesn't have fewer problems; they have a different vantage point from which to view those problems. They're thinking from heaven down rather than from earth up.

This is what it means to walk on earth while living from heaven; to make decisions, face challenges, and navigate relationships from your seated position with Christ, not from the limitations of your circumstances. You physically occupy this world while spiritually operating from another realm. The kingdom of God truly is within you, governing your thoughts, shaping your responses, determining your perspective.

The pattern connects you to heavenly realities. Hear God's Word about the exchange that took place at the cross, and you're hearing about what exists in the unseen realm. Believe those truths despite contrary circumstances, and you're thinking from heaven's perspective. Speak declarations based on God's promises rather than natural limitations, and you're operating from your seated position with Christ. Receive by faith what grace has provided, and you're accessing your spiritual inheritance in the heavenly places.

This is why the pattern produces life and peace, as Romans 8:6 promises. You're not trapped in carnal thinking that can only see problems and limitations. You're not dominated by circumstances that seem bigger than God's promises. Instead, you're spiritually minded, thinking from heaven's perspective, living from your true position in Christ, accessing resources that exist in the unseen realm but produce very real results in the natural world.

The beautiful part is that you don't have to work at becoming heavenly-minded as if it's another goal to achieve. As you continue in the pattern you've learned throughout this book, hearing God's Word, believing His promises, speaking His truth, and receiving His provision, you are automatically setting your mind on things above. This is what being spiritually minded looks like in practical, daily life.

You're not adding another layer of spiritual activity to your already busy schedule. You're simply discovering that what you've been doing all along, this simple pattern of engaging with God's Word through faith, is exactly what Scripture describes as setting your mind on things above and being spiritually minded. And as you continue in this lifestyle, you'll experience more and more of the life and peace that comes from thinking God's thoughts after Him, seeing from His perspective, and living from your true position seated with Christ in heavenly places.

Dealing with Seasons

Abundant life doesn't mean every season will feel abundant. There will be times of testing, waiting, and apparent setbacks. These seasons are opportunities to prove the reality of your faith and see God's faithfulness in new ways.

In Seasons of Testing: *Faith under fire*, you are called back to basics. Hear God's Word more intensively, believe His promises despite contrary evidence, speak His truth more deliberately, and receive His grace for endurance.

In Seasons of Waiting: Believing for something that hasn't manifested yet? Remember Abraham's example. Use the waiting time to let God's Word strengthen your faith and prepare you for what He has planned.

In Seasons of Loss: Grief and disappointment will come, but don't abandon God's truth. Instead, let His Word comfort you, His promises sustain you, and His love heal you. Some of your greatest growth will come during difficult seasons.

The Eternal Perspective

Remember that the abundant life you're experiencing now is just a preview of what's coming in eternity. Every healing is a glimpse of your resurrection body, every provision is a taste of heaven's abundance, and every moment of peace is a foretaste of eternal rest.

This perspective keeps you from becoming discouraged when you don't see the complete manifestation of every promise immediately. You're living in the "already but not yet," already blessed with every spiritual blessing in heavenly places, but not yet experiencing the fullness of what's coming.

Your Legacy

As you consistently live the abundant life, you're creating a legacy that extends far beyond your lifetime. Your children and grandchildren will be blessed by the faith foundation you're establishing. People whose lives you touch will carry the influence of your example.

Moving Forward

The journey of living as God's new creation never ends. There will always be new areas to grow in, fresh challenges to face with faith, and deeper levels of God's truth to discover. But you now have the tools you need: hear His Word, believe His promises, speak His truth, and receive His abundance.

Make this a lifestyle, not just a temporary emphasis. Let the hear-believe-speak-receive pattern become so natural that you do it without thinking. Fill your mind with Scripture, your mouth with praise, and your heart with expectation for all God has in store for you.

The abundant life Jesus promised is not just possible, it's your inheritance as His new creation. Walk in it, enjoy it, and let it overflow to bless everyone around you.

Bridging the Gap: Living the Abundant Life - Your Ongoing Journey

The abundant life Jesus promised isn't a future hope or something you achieve through effort. It's your present inheritance that you access by consistently living the hear-believe-speak-receive pattern. As this becomes your lifestyle, you naturally think from your heavenly position seated with Christ rather than from earthly limitations, and God's abundance overflows into every area of your life and to everyone around you.

The thief does not come except to steal, and to kill, and to destroy. I have come that they may have life, and that they may have it more abundantly.

—*John 10:10*

LIVING THE PATTERN

You now understand God's pattern for walking in grace and living as His new creation. The journey we've taken together through these pages isn't just information; it's a transformation waiting to happen in your life.

You are not who you used to be. The old person who struggled with sin, shame, sickness, lack, and limitation was crucified with Christ 2,000 years ago. In God's eternal perspective, that person is dead and gone forever. You are now a new creation with a new nature, new possibilities, and new access to everything God has provided through Jesus' finished work.

The gap between your eternal identity and your earthly experience is bridged by grace through the simple but powerful pattern we've explored: hear God's Word, believe His promises, speak His truth, and receive what He's provided. This isn't a formula to master but a way of life to embrace, a continuous process of letting Scripture transform you from the inside out.

Remember these key truths as you move forward:

The Word Does the Work: You don't have to strive, perform, or earn God's blessings. His Word is alive and powerful, and it effectively works in you as you believe. Your job is to position yourself to receive what grace provides.

Consistency Matters More Than Perfection: You won't walk flawlessly in your new identity from day one. There will be setbacks, moments when you respond from the old nature, and times when faith feels difficult. This is part of the learning process, not evidence of failure.

Grace Covers Everything: When you fall short, grace is there to lift you up. When faith wavers, grace provides strength to believe. When circumstances seem contrary, grace bridges the gap between promise and fulfillment.

God's Timing Is Perfect: Some promises manifest quickly, others take time to develop. Your job isn't to figure out the timeline but to keep trusting the process. What God has promised, He will perform.

Transformation Affects Others: As you grow in your new creation identity, the abundant life naturally overflows to bless your family, friends, and community. You become a demonstration of God's goodness and a source of encouragement to others.

The story of Cornelius that we've followed throughout this book shows us that transformation happens when we position ourselves to hear God's truth, believe it over our circumstances, speak it with our mouths, and receive it by faith. His entire household was saved and filled with the Holy Spirit because they followed this pattern together.

You can experience the same kind of breakthrough in your life. Whether you need healing, provision, restored relationships, freedom from addiction, or peace in the midst of a storm, God's Word has the answer, and the hear-believe-speak-receive pattern is how you access it.

Take what you've learned and put it into practice immediately. Choose the scriptures that speak to your current needs. Begin hearing them daily, believing them despite contrary circumstances, speaking them over your life, and receiving them by faith. Let this become your new way of living.

Jesus loves you so much that He gave everything to make you new. He bore your sickness, carried your sorrows, took your poverty, and defeated your enemies so you could walk in health, joy, abundance, and victory. All of this is already yours; now learn to live in it.

Keep hearing, keep believing, keep speaking, and keep receiving. Let God's Word transform you into the person He created you to be. Walk in the freedom of your new creation identity, and watch as His grace makes all things new in your life.

The abundant life Jesus promised is not just possible, it's your inheritance. Live it, enjoy it, and let it overflow to bless everyone around you.

Your journey as God's new creation has just begun. Make it count for eternity.

Scripture Memory Verses for Daily Confession

These scripture confessions are examples to help you get started in speaking God's Word over your life. As you continue in the hear-believe-speak-receive pattern, the Holy Spirit will reveal other truths from God's Word that are specific to your circumstances and needs. Let Him guide you to the scriptures that will build your faith and transform your heart.

Forgiveness & Justification

> **2 Corinthians 5:17** - "If anyone is in Christ, he is a new creation; old things have passed away; behold, all things have become new." **Confess:** "I am a new creation in Christ; old things have passed away; all things have become new."

> **Romans 8:1** - "There is therefore now no condemnation to those who are in Christ Jesus." **Confess:** "There is no condemnation for me because I am in Christ Jesus."

> **2 Corinthians 5:21** - "For He made Him who knew no sin to be sin for us, that we might become the righteousness of God in Him." **Confess:** "I am the righteousness of God in Christ."

> **Romans 5:1** - "Therefore, having been justified by faith, we have peace with God through our Lord Jesus Christ." **Confess:** "I have been justified by faith; I have peace with God through Jesus Christ."

> **Ephesians 1:7** - "In Him we have redemption through His blood, the forgiveness of sins, according to the riches of His grace." **Confess:** "I have redemption through Christ's blood; my sins are forgiven according to the riches of His grace."

> **Colossians 1:13-14** - "He has delivered us from the power of darkness and conveyed us into the kingdom of the Son of His

love, in whom we have redemption through His blood, the forgiveness of sins." **Confess:** "I have been delivered from darkness and brought into Christ's kingdom; I have redemption and forgiveness through His blood."

Health & Wholeness

Isaiah 53:5 - "But He was wounded for our transgressions, He was bruised for our iniquities; the chastisement for our peace was upon Him, and by His stripes we are healed." **Confess:** "By His stripes I am healed."

Psalm 103:2-3 - "Bless the Lord, O my soul, and forget not all His benefits: who forgives all your iniquities, who heals all your diseases." **Confess:** "The Lord forgives all my sins and heals all my diseases."

3 John 1:2 - "Beloved, I pray that you may prosper in all things and be in health, just as your soul prospers." **Confess:** "I prosper in all things and am in health as my soul prospers."

Matthew 8:17 - "He Himself took our infirmities and bore our sicknesses." **Confess:** "Jesus took my infirmities and bore my sicknesses."

1 Peter 2:24 - "Who Himself bore our sins in His own body on the tree, that we, having died to sins, might live for righteousness—by whose stripes you were healed." **Confess:** "Jesus bore my sins in His body; by His stripes I am healed."

Psalm 91:1-2 - "He who dwells in the secret place of the Most High shall abide under the shadow of the Almighty. I will say of the Lord, 'He is my refuge and my fortress; my God, in Him I will trust.'" **Confess:** "I dwell in the secret place of the Most High and abide under His shadow; the Lord is my refuge and fortress."

Psalm 34:17 - "The righteous cry out, and the Lord hears, and delivers them out of all their troubles." **Confess:** "The Lord hears my cry and delivers me out of all my troubles."

2 Thessalonians 3:3 - "But the Lord is faithful, who will establish you and guard you from the evil one." **Confess:** "The Lord is faithful; He establishes me and guards me from the evil one."

Psalm 121:7-8 - "The Lord shall preserve you from all evil; He shall preserve your soul. The Lord shall preserve your going out and your coming in from this time forth, and even forevermore." **Confess:** "The Lord preserves me from all evil; He preserves my soul and watches over my coming and going."

Isaiah 54:17 - "No weapon formed against you shall prosper, and every tongue which rises against you in judgment you shall condemn. This is the heritage of the servants of the Lord, and their righteousness is from Me, says the Lord." **Confess:** "No weapon formed against me shall prosper; this is my heritage as a servant of the Lord."

Provision & Prosperity

Philippians 4:19 - "And my God shall supply all your need according to His riches in glory by Christ Jesus." **Confess:** "My God supplies all my needs according to His riches in glory."

2 Corinthians 9:8 - "And God is able to make all grace abound toward you, that you, always having all sufficiency in all things, may have an abundance for every good work." **Confess:** "God makes all grace abound toward me; I have all sufficiency in all things and abundance for every good work."

Psalm 23:1 - "The Lord is my shepherd; I shall not want." **Confess:** "The Lord is my shepherd; I shall not lack anything."

2 Corinthians 9:10-11 - "Now may He who supplies seed to the sower, and bread for food, supply and multiply the seed you have sown and increase the fruits of your righteousness, while you are enriched in everything for all liberality." **Confess:** "God supplies seed to me and multiplies what I have sown; I am enriched in everything for all generosity."

Matthew 6:33 - "But seek first the kingdom of God and His righteousness, and all these things shall be added to you." **Confess:** "As I seek first God's kingdom and His righteousness, all these things are added to me."

Philippians 4:7 - "And the peace of God, which surpasses all understanding, will guard your hearts and minds through Christ Jesus." **Confess:** "The peace of God guards my heart and mind through Christ Jesus."

John 14:27 - "Peace I leave with you, My peace I give to you; not as the world gives do I give to you. Let not your heart be troubled, neither let it be afraid." **Confess:** "Jesus gives me His peace; my heart is not troubled or afraid."

Nehemiah 8:10 - "Do not sorrow, for the joy of the Lord is your strength." **Confess:** "The joy of the Lord is my strength."

Isaiah 26:3 - "You will keep him in perfect peace, whose mind is stayed on You, because he trusts in You." **Confess:** "God keeps me in perfect peace because my mind is stayed on Him and I trust in Him."

Romans 15:13 - "Now may the God of hope fill you with all joy and peace in believing, that you may abound in hope by the power of the Holy Spirit." **Confess:** "The God of hope fills me with all joy and peace in believing; I abound in hope by the power of the Holy Spirit."

Answer to Prayer

Matthew 21:22 - "And whatever things you ask in prayer, believing, you will receive." **Confess:** "Whatever I ask in prayer, believing, I will receive."

1 John 5:14-15 - "Now this is the confidence that we have in Him, that if we ask anything according to His will, He hears us. And if we know that He hears us, whatever we ask, we know that we have the petitions that we have asked of Him."
Confess: "I have confidence that when I ask according to God's will, He hears me; I have the petitions I have asked of Him."

John 14:13-14 - "And whatever you ask in My name, that I will do, that the Father may be glorified in the Son. If you ask anything in My name, I will do it." **Confess:** "Whatever I ask in Jesus' name, He will do it."

Mark 11:24 - "Therefore I say to you, whatever things you ask when you pray, believe that you receive them, and you will have them." **Confess:** "When I pray, I believe I receive what I ask, and I will have it."

1 Peter 3:12 - "For the eyes of the Lord are on the righteous, and His ears are open to their prayers." **Confess:** "The Lord's eyes are on me and His ears are open to my prayers."

Keep these truths in your heart, speak them with your mouth, and receive them by faith. This is how you walk as God's new creation.

APPENDIX: COMMON QUESTIONS AND CONCERNS

As you engage with the hear-believe-speak-receive pattern, you may find yourself wrestling with some questions or concerns. That's natural and healthy. Here are the most common objections we've encountered, along with biblical responses.

"Doesn't this promote passivity? What about spiritual discipline and obedience?"

This is perhaps the most common concern, and it's understandable. When we emphasize that God's Word does the work and transformation flows from receiving rather than striving, it can sound like we're promoting spiritual laziness.

But here's what's crucial to understand: there's a massive difference between passivity and rest. Passivity says, "I don't need to do anything." Rest says, "I'm positioning myself to receive what God is doing."

The hear-believe-speak-receive pattern is not passive. It requires:

- **Active hearing** - deliberately exposing yourself to God's Word
- **Active believing** - choosing to trust God's truth over circumstances
- **Active speaking** - declaring God's Word over your situation
- **Active receiving** - positioning yourself in faith to receive what He's provided

This is far from passive! But it's also far from the Old Covenant approach of trying to generate righteousness through human effort.

Consider again Philippians 2:12-13: "Work out your own salvation with fear and trembling; for it is God who works in you both to will and to do for His good pleasure." Notice the progression: God works in you, then you work out what He's worked in. You're not generating transformation through discipline. You're cooperating with what God is already doing through His Word and Spirit.

Sons and daughters actually work harder than servants, but from a completely different foundation. The servant strives in their own strength, trying to earn favor. The son works from the overflow of received love and grace, empowered by divine strength. Same activities (prayer, service, generosity, obedience), completely different power source.

When you engage the hear-believe-speak-receive pattern, you're not sitting back passively waiting for God to zap you with transformation. You're actively cooperating with how grace operates. You're positioning yourself in the stream of divine power rather than trying to generate power through human effort.

What About Medical Treatment?"

Some ask whether this teaching discourages medical care or suggests that believing God's Word means avoiding doctors. The answer is no. God's Word reveals spiritual truth about healing and wholeness, but we live in fallen bodies that break down and minds that struggle. Medical care—doctors, therapy, medication, surgery—is part of God's grace to us in a broken world.

Luke was a physician and traveled with Paul (Colossians 4:14). Paul himself advised Timothy to use wine for his stomach ailments (1 Timothy 5:23). The Bible doesn't pit faith against medicine; it recognizes both as gifts from God. Seeking medical treatment is wisdom, not a lack of faith. Ignoring serious symptoms isn't faith; it's presumption.

This pattern works alongside medical care, not as a replacement for it. You can believe God's Word about healing while also taking prescribed medication. You can declare "by His stripes I am healed" while sitting in a doctor's office. You can trust God's provision while undergoing treatment. Faith and medicine aren't enemies; they're both tools God uses to care for His children in a fallen world.

"Isn't this just name-it-and-claim-it prosperity gospel?"

This concern usually arises because both false prosperity teaching and biblical faith involve speaking God's Word. But the similarities end there, and the differences are crucial.

The Counterfeit: "Name-It-Claim-It"

What's commonly called "name-it-and-claim-it" involves speaking desires and outcomes that aren't found in Scripture, then treating those words as if they have the power to create reality. People declare "I'm a millionaire," "I own a boat," "I'm a successful entrepreneur"—not because God promised these specific things, but because they want them.

This is closer to witchcraft and spellcasting than biblical faith. It treats words themselves as having magical power, as if speaking creates reality independent of God's will. It's attempting to engineer outcomes through the force of positive confession rather than receiving what God has already provided through Christ.

The focus is entirely wrong: What do I want? How can I get it? What words do I need to speak to make it happen?

The Biblical Pattern: Claiming God's Promises

The hear-believe-speak-receive pattern operates on an entirely different foundation. You're not making up declarations based on your desires. You're finding promises God has already made in Scripture and accessing what Christ has already provided through His finished work. Even Jesus Himself said, *"It is written."*

There's a massive difference between:

- "I declare I'm a millionaire" (not a biblical promise)
- "My God supplies all my needs according to His riches in glory" (Philippians 4:19 - an actual promise)

- Or between:
- "I claim a new car" (not found in Scripture)
- "By His stripes I am healed" (Isaiah 53:5, 1 Peter 2:24 - purchased at the cross)

The Key Distinctions:

False Name-It-Claim-It	Biblical Pattern
Speaks desires not found in Scripture	Speaks promises explicitly stated in God's Word
Treats words as having magic power	Recognizes that God's Word has inherent power
Focuses on what YOU want	Focuses on what GOD has provided
Seeks to manipulate God into giving	Receives what grace has already given
Makes faith a force you control	Makes faith a response to hearing God's truth
Uses God to get stuff	Seeks God and receives provision
Material prosperity is the PRIMARY goal	Knowing Christ is the goal; provision flows from that

"What if I do everything right and nothing happens?"

This question reveals a subtle but important misunderstanding: you're not doing the pattern to make God move. You're engaging the pattern to cooperate with what God is already doing.

But let's be honest about the tension: sometimes you faithfully hear God's Word, genuinely believe His promises, consistently speak His truth, position yourself to receive... and the specific outcome you're praying for doesn't manifest the way or when you expected.

Does this mean the pattern failed? Absolutely not.

Here's what the hear-believe-speak-receive pattern guarantees:

What it ALWAYS produces:

- Faith that comes from hearing God's Word (Romans 10:17)

- Peace that surpasses understanding (Philippians 4:7)

- Confidence in God's goodness, even when you don't understand His timing

- A renewed mind that sees from heaven's perspective (Romans 12:2)

- Trust in God's character that transcends circumstances

- The assurance that all things work together for good (Romans 8:28)

What it doesn't guarantee:

- Your specific timeline

- Your preferred method

- Your exact outcome

- Immunity from trials

- Freedom from mystery

Remember, even Jesus prayed, "let this cup pass from Me" in Gethsemane, yet the outcome was crucifixion. But through that apparent defeat came the greatest victory in history. Sometimes what we receive is different from what we asked for, but it's always what we need.

Abraham waited at least 15 years between God's promise and Isaac's birth. During that time, the pattern anchored his faith. He was "strengthened in faith, giving glory to God, and being fully convinced that what He had promised He was also able to perform" (Romans 4:20-21). The pattern kept him anchored while he waited for manifestation.

The goal isn't to get the pattern "right" so God will perform. The goal is to position yourself to receive what God is doing—whatever that looks like. Trust that He's faithful, His Word is true, and His timing is perfect even when it's mysterious.